ScottForesman
In Charge

MW00358976

MOYA BRENNAN
University of California Santa Barbara Extension
Santa Barbara, California

BARBARA R. DENMAN
Prince George's County Adult Education Program
Prince George's County, Maryland

ScottForesman

With thanks and appreciation to friends and neighbors in Ann Arbor, Santa Barbara, and Oxford for their support and in particular to Diana Paine, ESL Consultant, for insightful suggestions, assistance, and reviews.

Moya Brennan

I would like to thank all of the people who generously contributed their time and their ideas to this project: Shirley Denman, Harry Denman, Cynthia Denman, Richard Denman, Mark Brice, Charles McNamara, Jeanne Cablish, Leticia Flores, and Alex and Teddy. I would also like to thank Diane Pinkley and Tim Collins at ScottForesman for their help, patience, and support.

This book is dedicated to my family.

Barbara R. Denman

CONSULTING REVIEWERS

Anna Marie Amudi, *Dhahran Ahliyya Schools*
Dammam, Saudi Arabia

Marilyn Bach, *New York City Public Schools*
New York City, New York

Bonnie Baker, *Paulsboro School District*
Paulsboro, New Jersey

Tracy Caldwell Gavilanes, *Pontificia Universidad Católica del Ecuador*
Quito, Ecuador

Estrella Cases, *Florida Atlantic University*
Boca Raton, Florida

Antonio Cervellino, *Chilean Ministry of Education*
Santiago, Chile

Manuel C. R. Dos Santos, *ELT Author/Consultant*
Curitiba, Brazil

Miriam García de Bermúdez, *Universidad de Costa Rica*
San Jose, Costa Rica

Stephen Gudgel, *Institute of North American Studies*
Barcelona, Spain

Mario Herrera Salazar, *Director, Language Center of the Normal Superior of Nuevo Leon*
Monterrey, Mexico

Carlos Alberto Hoffmann de Mendonça, *Colegio Pedro II*
Rio de Janeiro, Brazil

Fang-Lian Liao, *Santa Monica College*
Santa Monica, California

Jacqueline Lovelace, *Dallas Independent School District*
Dallas, Texas

Titika Magaliou, *Athens College*
Athens, Greece

Ricardo F. Marzo, *Director, ELS-Peru*
Lima, Peru

Will E. McCarther, *Wright State University*
Dayton, Ohio

David Miller-Siegel, *Minnesota State University*
Akita, Japan

Deborah Monroe, *Glendale Community College*
Glendale, California

Lourdes Montoro, B.A. (English Philology), M.A. (Translation) *Escola Oficial d'Idiomes*
Barcelona, Spain

Jose Javier Preciado Ceseña, *Universidad Nacional Autonoma de Mexico, Centro Universitario Mexico*
Mexico City, Mexico

Issam Safady, *University of Jordan, English Department*
Amman, Jordan

Carol Speranza, *Teacher Training Institute*
Stara Zagora, Bulgaria

Darleen Videen Lennan, *Florence Unified School District*
Florence, Arizona

Christine Zaher, M.A., M. Ed., *The American University in Cairo*
Cairo, Egypt

CONTENTS

- To speculate about the future, present, and past
- To invite participation
- To ask for clarification

 GETTING TO KNOW YOU!

As you progress in your English and communication skills in this class, you will share information about yourself and your culture with your teacher and classmates, as well as gain knowledge from them. Begin by introducing yourself, finding out about your course, and getting acquainted with your classmates.

EXERCISE 1: *The Big Picture*

Work with your teacher and classmates to find out about the topics in the chart. Ask and answer questions as necessary. Be as specific as possible. Write down the information you need to remember on a sheet of paper.

Classroom Concerns	Classroom Language	Study Strategies
1. homework policy 2. dates, types of exams 3. compositions 4. grading policy 5. course objective 6. personal goals	1. clarification 2. correction 3. agreement/disagreement 4. explanation 5. comparison	habits and tips: vocabulary grammar listening reading writing speaking problem-solving

EXERCISE 2: *Your Classmates' Facts. . . .*

A. *Work with a partner. Take turns choosing topics from the box and asking and answering questions about them. Find out as much as you can about your partner. Take notes.*

hometown	hobbies	favorite writer	bad habits
nationality	family	favorite dessert	birthday
car	skills	favorite music	personality
holiday	sports	favorite subjects	computer

B. *Work in small groups. Take turns telling your new classmates about yourself and your partner from part **A**. Include the information you learned in part **A** and then tell how you and your partner are similar and different.*

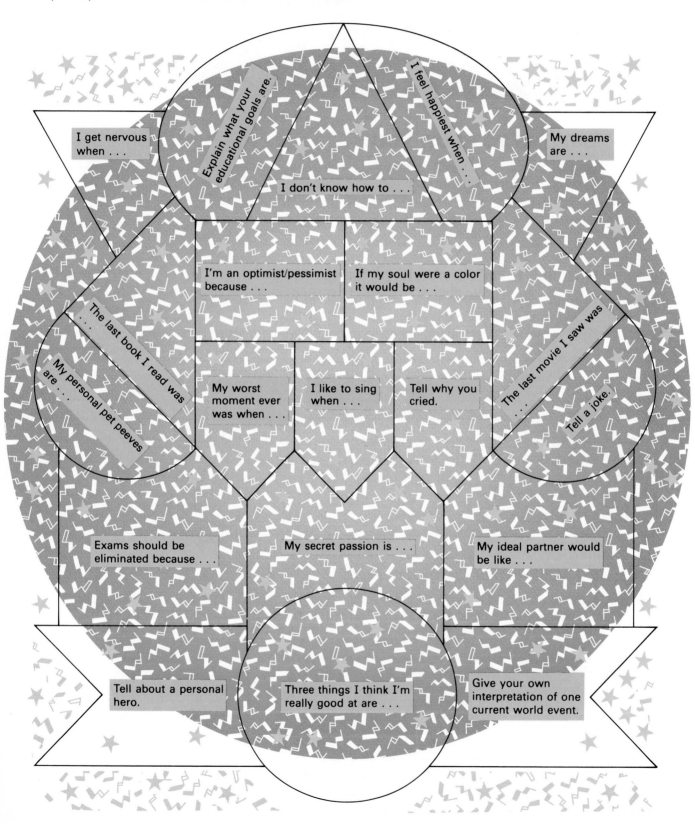

EXERCISE 3: *And Feelings....*

Work in groups. Take turns closing your eyes and placing a finger on one of the spaces in the diagram. Open your eyes, read the question or instruction in the space you chose and carry out the task. Your partners may ask you for clarification or additional information.

I get nervous when . . .

Explain what your educational goals are.

I feel happiest when . . .

My dreams are . . .

I don't know how to . . .

I'm an optimist/pessimist because . . .

If my soul were a color it would be . . .

The last book I read was . . .

My personal pet peeves are . . .

My worst moment ever was when . . .

I like to sing when . . .

Tell why you cried.

The last movie I saw was . . .

Tell a joke.

Exams should be eliminated because . . .

My secret passion is . . .

My ideal partner would be like . . .

Tell about a personal hero.

Three things I think I'm really good at are . . .

Give your own interpretation of one current world event.

UNIT 1 A Way with Words

 THINK ABOUT IT!

A. Do you have a way with words, that is, are you good at communicating? What were probably your first words as a baby? your first words in English? What were the first words in English that you heard? understood? said? Fill in the table. Then compare your answers to a partner's.

The first words I:	**heard**	**understood**	**said**
first language:			
second language:			
third language:			

B. Try to tell your partner something without using words. Did your partner understand you? What did you do if he or she didn't? Compare your strategies with those of the class.

 TALK IT OVER!

A. Sometimes humans find it hard to get their message across. Do animals have the same problem? How do animals communicate?

B. Scientists who study animal behavior say that our interpretation of animal communication is often subjective and too simple. Do you agree that we often see things such as animal behavior only from our human point of view? Why or why not?

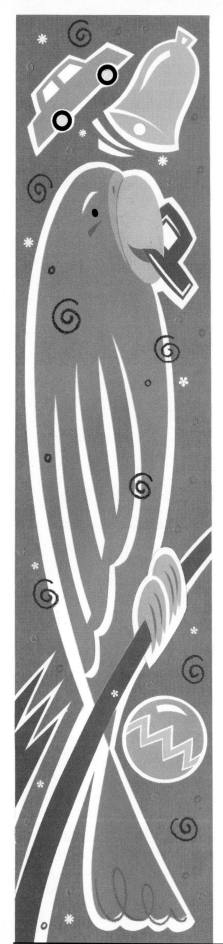

 READ ABOUT IT!

Skimming for Ideas and Scanning for Details

As you know, both skimming and scanning are reading strategies in which we read a text very quickly. The difference between them lies in the purpose. We skim to find main ideas and key concepts, and we scan to find details. Quickly look over the article about Alex the parrot and answer the questions.

A. Skim the article. Write the number(s) of the paragraphs that give the information on the lines.

1. the name of Alex's teacher   paragraph _____

2. the words he can say   paragraph _____

3. the teaching method used   paragraph _____

B. Scan the article. Circle the letter(s) of the correct answer(s). Discuss your answers with a partner.

1. The article about Alex has
- **a.** scientific words.
- **b.** everyday language.
- **c.** headings and subheadings.
- **d.** long dialogues.

2. This magazine article is written for
- **a.** anthropology students.
- **b.** linguists and language teachers.
- **c.** people interested in wild animals.
- **d.** pet shop owners.

3. Ethologist Pepperberg is studying
- **a.** tropical birds.
- **b.** biochemistry.
- **c.** animal behavior.
- **d.** foreign languages.

4. After reading this article, we will know
- **a.** how to conduct a similar experiment.
- **b.** what Alex can do and say.
- **c.** all the details of the experiment.
- **d.** some interesting facts about parrots' skills.

5. The researcher's hypothesis is that
- **a.** parrots like to talk to humans.
- **b.** parrots can understand the meaning of words.
- **c.** parrots can do mathematics.
- **d.** parrots only mimic.

6. The results show that
- **a.** Alex sometimes seems to think like a human.
- **b.** parrots are as intelligent as children.
- **c.** parrots can speak English very well.
- **d.** Alex says what he thinks.

7. Alex correctly identifies objects more than
- **a.** forty percent of the time.
- **b.** sixty percent of the time.
- **c.** eighty percent of the time.
- **d.** ninety percent of the time.

8. A doubt raised about Pepperberg's research is that
- **a.** Pepperberg's records are not accurate.
- **b.** Alex is secretly given the answers beforehand.
- **c.** Alex's words do not show an intent to communicate.
- **d.** Alex's language is not complex enough.

This Bird Has a Way with Words
by Douglas Starr

Ethologist Irene Pepperberg is discovering that a parrot can not only mimic people but also learn the meaning of words.

Irene Pepperberg holds a round tray in front of a parrot she has named Alex. On the tray are five objects, three of them keys.

"How many keys?" asked Pepperberg, a researcher in the anthropology department at Northwestern University, in Evanston,
5 Illinois.

"Fiiiive!" says Alex.

"No, not how many toys, how many keys?"

"Thrrrree!"

"Good, Alex."

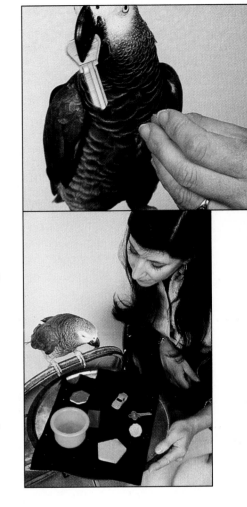

10   Very good, indeed. Alex is an African Grey parrot and for the most part just an ordinary bird. But, in many ways, Alex is a rare bird, for he has demonstrated the kind of mental abilities that scientists once thought only humans possessed.

Alex names objects, like "walnut," "paper," and "corn." He
15 identifies colors and shapes. He perceives quantities up to six. He says "want" when he desires something, and "no" when he does not. He understands concepts such as "same" and "different" and applies them to objects he has never seen before. "People didn't feel parrots could do anything other than
20 mimic," says Pepperberg, an ethologist. "We've shown they're capable of abstract thought."

To teach Alex, Pepperberg used a form of training called "referential rewards." Rather than give Alex a nut each time he said something, she'd only give it when he specifically said "nut."
25 If he said "water" she would give him water. Human parents teach some parts of language by giving toddlers what they ask for. Pepperberg hoped that a similar system would help Alex grasp the meaning of words, not just their sounds.

"The idea was to correlate the object and the word," says
30 Pepperberg. "If he said, 'cork,' we'd give him a cork—not a piece of food."

Alex seemed to quickly learn nouns such as "paper," "key," and "cork," and color names such as "red," "green," and "yellow." Tests showed that Alex didn't just mimic. For example,
35 Pepperberg would show Alex an object, such as a green wooden peg or a red paper triangle. More than eighty percent of the time, Alex would correctly describe the object and color, even if he had never seen that particular object before (he might, however, have previously seen a wooden peg of a different size or color). In
40 short, Alex was able to take a small number of labels and correctly recombine them in novel situations.

A greater skill involved his mastery of "same" and "different"—notions that are more abstract than color and shape. Pepperberg can show Alex two objects (for example, a green wooden square
45 versus a red wooden square) and ask, "What's different?" Alex will reply, "Color!" Even with objects he has never seen before, Alex responds correctly about eighty percent of the time.

Some psychologists see warning flags in Pepperberg's research. Herbert Terrace, professor of psychology at Columbia
50 University says that even if Alex is using words, it's wrong to call it language. "One aspect of language is an *intent* to communicate," he says. "Like, 'Hey, I just saw a blue paper square!'" This animal [Alex] is just working for rewards."

But Pepperberg says working with the feathered orator has
55 already changed how many people regard animals. "Animals in the wild are not automatons," she says. "They process information and make decisions. Their communication may be much more complex than we thought."

How complex? Ask Alex.

DISCUSSION

1. Is animal communication research valuable?

2. How can we know and trust the results of scientific experiments?

3. Should animals be used in laboratory research? Why or why not?

Figuring Out the Meaning of Words from Context

As we read we often encounter unfamiliar words. Many times we can figure out the meaning of these words by looking at other phrases or sentences in the text. Nearby phrases or sentences may contain a synonym or paraphrase of the concept we need or there may be an explanation or example that helps us clarify meaning. Sometimes determining even the part of speech of the unknown word can give us useful clues.

EXERCISE 1: *Meaning from Context*

A. *These explanations correspond in meaning to words in the article. Find the words they define and write them on the lines.*

1. _____ : a person who studies how animals behave and think

2. _____ : a form of training in which the learner is given something when he specifically says the word for it

3. _____ : to match or connect things, for example, an object and a word

4. _____ : an animal or person who is **not** able to process information and make decisions

B. *Find the word in the article and figure out its meaning from the context. Write a synonym or short definition on a sheet of paper. Work without a dictionary. What in the context helped you figure out each word?*

1. perceive *(line 15)*
2. mimic *(line 20)*
3. capable *(line 21)*
4. rewards *(line 23)*
5. grasp *(line 28)*
6. process *(line 56)*

WORD FOR WORD!

English has many idioms—expressions that add interest and color to the language. Idioms are frequently used in magazine and newspaper articles and on radio and television, as well as in everyday speech. One large group of idioms has to do with animals.

goose:

worms:

rat:

hog:

EXERCISE 2: *A Whale of a Job!*

A. *Look at the words and expressions in dark type and match them to their meanings. Use the context to help you. Write the number on the line.*

1. The escaped prisoner led the police in a **wild goose chase** all over town. Twelve police officers looked for him for over seven hours, and they couldn't catch him!
2. Marcia is a real **bookworm**! She always has a book in her purse, and she reads at every opportunity.
3. I think I should go to the doctor. I don't know what's wrong with me—I just feel **dog-tired** all the time.
4. Frank told me he was really getting tired of all the competition and stress involved with his job. He said he was thinking about quitting the **rat race** and retiring.
5. Dolores can't come to the phone right now. She's taking a little **cat-nap.** She didn't get to bed until very late.
6. Just look at that car in the middle of the road! Nobody can pass on either side. That driver is a real **road hog!**

_____ **a.** compulsive reader

_____ **b.** constant competition

_____ **c.** takes up more of the street than necessary

_____ **d.** rest, sleep

_____ **e.** useless activity

_____ **f.** exhausted

B. *Work with a partner. Look at the animal idioms and come up with a possible meaning for each one. Next make a sentence with each idiom, illustrating your meaning. Then compare your ideas with the meanings given in a dictionary. Were your ideas similar? very different? Why do you think so?*

birdbrain
black sheep
crocodile tears
fishy
goose bumps

SPEAK OUT!

Convincing

To convince someone effectively, it is helpful to speak with authority, to use facts to support opinions, and to present ideas clearly, speaking with a firm tone of voice.

Expressing Doubt and Surprise

When we listen to an expert we are often surprised by the new information we learn. Sometimes we don't even believe it! When we express our doubt or surprise, the expert often gives us more information to convince us.

In the conversation, what are the facts Don used to convince Josh that whales are endangered? that whales are worth saving? What expressions did Josh use to show his surprise at Don's information? What expressions did he use to show doubt? Underline them in the conversation.

DON: Hi Josh! That's a great T-shirt you're wearing!

JOSH: Thanks, Don. It was a gift. I never thought I'd wear a "Save the Whales" shirt, but here I am! And I don't know anything about whales!

DON: Well, did you know that whales are in danger of extinction?

JOSH: Really?

DON: Yes! They are really such beautiful creatures and we know very little about them. Studies show they've been on this earth longer than we have, but too many are being hunted each year and chemicals in the ocean are endangering them, too. Scientists do know they have very large brains—bigger than ours.

JOSH: Is that a fact?

DON: And research shows they seem to communicate by singing.

JOSH: You don't say! Sort of love songs?

DON: Well, maybe. It seems that only males sing, so it could be to attract mates. The songs change a little every year, so they might be a record of their experiences.

JOSH: Wow! That's really interesting.

DON: You know, in the old days, sailors heard the songs and thought mermaids were singing!

JOSH: You're kidding!

DON: No—there are legends and poems about mermaids. But now we have all sorts of high-tech equipment to record whales and follow them around. One cetologist recorded a song for twenty-two hours and then just gave up!

JOSH: That's amazing!

DON: Experts think their songs can be heard over 750 miles.

JOSH: I can hardly believe that!

DON: The scientists who work with whales feel that they do try to communicate with us.

JOSH: Well, I can't really imagine what a whale would have to say to me!

EXERCISE 3: *Of Course It's True!*

*Choose three of the statements and convince a partner that they are true. Your partner will express surprise or doubt depending on how convincing you are. Circle **T** if your partner convinces you the statement is true. Circle **F** if you are not convinced by your partner's explanation.*

1. Elephants communicate by making throat noises.	**T**	**F**
2. Bees dance to show other bees where the honey is.	**T**	**F**
3. Sharks cannot stop swimming or they will sink.	**T**	**F**
4. Parrots can learn Chinese.	**T**	**F**
5. Male spiders wave their legs to attract female spiders.	**T**	**F**
6. Ants give off chemicals to tell others about food.	**T**	**F**

bee: **shark:**   **spider:**   **ants:**

 EXERCISE 4: *Really? Really!*

*What areas are **you** an expert in? Think of your experience with hobbies, animals, cars, learning languages, etc. Work with a partner. Take turns telling surprising things about areas you know well, supporting your statements with facts, and expressing doubt and surprise.*

(G) FIGURE IT OUT!

Talking About Actions in the Present

Review the ways we talk about actions in the present by going back to the article about Alex on pages 5 and 6. Underline all the examples of ways to talk about the present. Identify the tenses and their formation.

is discovering	**present progressive**	***be* + verb + *ing***

 EXERCISE 5: *No Time Like the Present*

Use your underlined examples to answer the questions. Circle the correct answer. Discuss your answers with a partner.

1. We use this tense to describe an action occurring at a present moment or to talk about things that change.

    a. simple present   **b.** present progressive   **c.** present perfect

2. We use this tense to describe an action that happens regularly or to comment on a procedure involving a series of actions.

    a. simple present   **b.** present progressive   **c.** present perfect

3. We use this tense to talk of a recently completed action or to emphasize that we expect an action to continue.

    a. simple present   **b.** present progressive   **c.** present perfect

EXERCISE 6: *From Whales to Elephants*

Read the text and then fill in the tense you think best completes each sentence. Write the correct form of the verb on a sheet of paper.

Scientist Katy Payne **(1. work)** _____ for most of her life on the songs of whales. Recently she **(2. become)** _____ interested in how elephants **(3. communicate)** _____. From her experience with whales she **(4. know)** _____ that animals, such as bats and porpoises **(5. communicate)** _____ with sounds that **(6. be)** _____ above the range of the human ear—ultrasound. Using her special equipment she **(7. discover)** _____ that elephants produce very low but loud sounds, below the range of our ears—infrasound. She **(8. examine)** _____ the different types of calls to try to understand the messages. Other researchers **(9. find)** _____ that elephants can tell other elephants over ninety miles away about the dangers of hunters. Many other animals as well as elephants **(10. develop)** _____ ways to warn each other about human beings—the very species that needs to learn from them the most.

LISTEN TO THIS!

While we want to understand and be understood in our communications with everyone most of the time, occasionally we prefer a more private exchange limited to one or two people. Sometimes we invent words with special personal meanings or use initials to communicate a whole sentence or idea. For example, the initials LDA might stand for "Leave Dad alone!" Do you know of any private words, initials, or signals used in your own family? Did you use any words in a special way as a child? Share an anecdote with a partner.

EXERCISE 7: *Idioglossia*

A. *Listen to the information about the Kennedy sisters and decide if the sentences are true or false. Write T for true or F for false on the lines.*

1. _____ The Kennedy sisters are speech therapists.

2. _____ Virginia and Grace speak a secret language that nobody else can understand.

3. _____ In addition to their own language, the girls understand Italian and German.

4. _____ Twin languages develop when their speakers have too much social contact with other children.

5. _____ Idioglossia is extremely rare.

6. _____ The Kennedy sisters learned sign language to communicate with their teachers.

B. *Based on your understanding of the monologue, write a definition of* **idioglossia** *on the lines.*

_____

_____

 ## SAY IT CLEARLY!

Distinguishing Time Orientation

Sometimes the difference in spoken English between the present participle and the past participle can be very small.

> I'm eat**ing** an apple.
> I've eat**en** an apple.

Usually we can figure out the time orientation from the context. Look at the sentence below. Is the action continuing or has it just finished? What words in the context helped you decide?

> -iŋ
> ⟶ ən
> -ən

> I've eaten an apple, but I'm still hungry!

EXERCISE 8: *Now or Then?*

Listen to the sentences and mark column 1 if the action is happening at the present moment and column 2 if the action has just ended. Pay careful attention to the verb endings.

	-ing	-en
1.	_____	_____
2.	_____	_____
3.	_____	_____
4.	_____	_____
5.	_____	_____
6.	_____	_____
7.	_____	_____
8.	_____	_____

EXERCISE 9: *Polly the Parrot*

Work with a partner. Student A reads the sentences on this page aloud and Student B the ones on page 12. As your partner reads, listen carefully, look at the pictures, and mark the one that best corresponds to each sentence. Write the number of the sentence in the box.

Student A

Sentence number one. Polly's taking the keys.
Sentence number two. Polly's fallen out of the cage!
Sentence number three. The scientist's given Polly a cracker.
Sentence number four. Polly's eating a nut.

Student B

Sentence number five. Polly's falling out of the cage!
Sentence number six. Polly's eaten a nut.
Sentence number seven. The scientist's giving Polly a cracker.
Sentence number eight. Polly's taken the keys.

 READ ABOUT IT!

Understanding a Bar Graph

A. Not all of the information we read comes from the text of magazines, newspapers, or books. We often find information represented in graphs and charts. One of the most common forms is the **bar graph,** which compares numbers by using bars of varying lengths to represent the numbers visually. When reading a bar graph, it is important to read the title, the headings on the columns and rows, and the numerical progressions.

B. Look at the bar graph on page 13. What is the title? What data does the graph compare? What unit of measurement do the numbers represent?

EXERCISE 10: *We're All Ears!*

Study the bar graph and then answer the questions on a sheet of paper.

1. What is the hearing range of grasshoppers?
2. Do fish hear sounds above 10 kHz?
3. Which group has the widest range of hearing?
4. Do moths hear the same range of sounds as bats do?
5. Which group is most limited in range of hearing?
6. Which groups distinguish sounds ranging from 0.1 to 1.0 kHz?

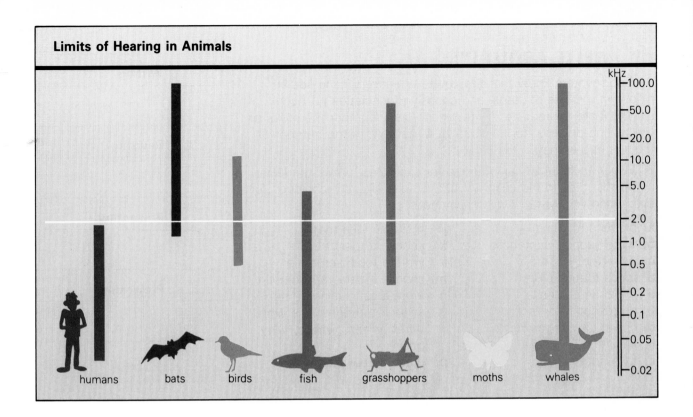

Limits of Hearing in Animals

 SPEAK OUT!

Changing the Topic of Conversation

Often, in our roles as listeners, we deal with people who have great knowledge or strong feelings about a subject. We may or may not share their interest. Politely indicating a lack of enthusiasm and a wish to change the topic of conversation is a useful social skill.

> FRED: Yes, the conference was quite interesting, but I feel we haven't given enough attention to the results of my latest research on the dance patterns of the honeybee as a form of communication. The aspects requiring further development include. . . .
>
> RAUL: You don't say. By the way, Fred, I was wondering if you knew when our next conference will be. Is it in February or March? My memory isn't what it was!

EXERCISE 11: *For a Change*

A. *Work with a partner. Read the example in the box. What expressions indicate a lack of interest and a desire to change the subject? Brainstorm a list of other ways to show lack of interest and other ways to change the subject. Share your ideas with the class.*

B. *Take turns beginning a conversation about each cue and politely interrupting to change the topic. Use your imaginations!*

1. range of hearing in animals
2. research on whale songs
3. a trip to the zoo
4. your own idea

WRITE ABOUT IT!

A. Good writers know that the key to effective writing lies in following a series of steps, and choosing techniques for each step that are appropriate to the writing task. Number the steps of the writing process from **1** (first) to **4** (last). Write the number on the line in the chart.

B. Which techniques can you use for each step? Write the letter under that step in the chart. Would you use all the techniques for everything you write? Why or why not?

_____ **Writing**	
_____ **Revising**	
_____ **Presenting**	
_____ **Prewriting**	

a. brainstorm ideas
b. write support sentences
c. write the final draft
d. focus the idea
e. make an outline
f. do research for facts
g. check the first draft
h. have someone read the draft
i. take notes

j. make an idea map
k. choose a topic
l. write a topic sentence
m. choose a paragraph function
n. write a concluding sentence
o. answer the questions **who, what, when, where, why, how**
p. present your paper

EXERCISE 12: *Getting Ready to Write*

Work with a partner. The two of you have to write an article about some form of animal communication for a student magazine. Work through the writing steps using either Alex the parrot or whales as your topic. When you have finished a rough draft, have another pair edit it for clarity, interest, grammar, spelling, and punctuation. Then write your final draft after you have received their comments.

EXERCISE 13: *My Way with Words*

Choose a topic of interest to you from the list and follow the writing steps necessary to develop your ideas. Show a partner your first draft. Revise your draft and submit your final copy to the class for reading and discussion.

1. the use of animals in laboratory experiments
2. the difficulties of communicating what you mean
3. the importance of animals to humans
4. your own idea

THINK ABOUT IT!

A biography is the story of the life of an individual. The subject of a biography may be living or dead, famous or not. A biography may cover the subject's whole life, or one event in which he or she was involved. Think of a biography you have read or seen on TV or in a movie. Did it cover the person's whole life or just a portion of it? Did you find the subject interesting? Why or why not?

Bill Cosby   *Carol Burnett*

Sonia Braga   *Yo Yo Ma*

Calvin Coolidge

TALK IT OVER!

Calvin Coolidge, the thirtieth President of the U.S., was known for being a man of few words. This famous story is told about him. One evening, at a Washington dinner party, the woman sitting next to Coolidge told him that she had heard that he usually had little to say. She said that she had made a bet that she could get him to say more than two words. Coolidge looked at her and replied, ''You lose.''

A. Do you think this anecdote is funny? Why? Do you know any humorous stories about famous people? Share an anecdote with the class.

B. What makes a person interesting? Make a list of the types of people you would like to read about. Compare your list with that of a classmate.

READ ABOUT IT!

Skimming for Organizational Patterns

When reading, it is helpful to figure out the organizational patterns the writer used. Quickly look over the article ''Comedy Under Control'' on page 16. Circle the letters of the correct answers.

1. The article is generally organized
   a. from the most important to the least important idea.
   b. by time.
   c. by topic.

2. The main purpose of the article is
   a. to explain a choice or decision.
   b. to persuade the reader.
   c. to tell a story.

Camille and Bill Cosby

Comedy Under Control
by Dan Goodgame

Bill Cosby may be the most beloved and best-paid entertainer in America, but he still works like a hungry journeyman. Cosby's drive, like much of his comic material, flows from his tough and tender upbringing in
5 a North Philadelphia housing project. His family endured poverty and prejudice but did not surrender to hopelessness. The Cosby home echoed with the sounds of people making up funny stories. Bill's mother Anna passed along her vivid and eccentric way of viewing the
10 commonplace. "She would tell me that if I swallowed the seeds along with the grapes, branches would grow out of my ears," Cosby recalls.

When Bill was only nine, his father, a welder, joined the Navy and left home, returning only occasionally at
15 first, and then not at all. The main man in his life became his maternal grandfather, Samuel Russell, who encouraged the yarns and jokes of his precocious grandson. At the end of a storytelling session, Russell would fish around in his cavernous back pocket, extract
20 a sock full of change, and reward the boy with the then princely sum of $.25. Already Cosby was learning that comedy could pay.

As a youngster, Cosby realized that he could make people like him, and get his way, by making them
25 laugh. At school he charmed the teachers. One of his elementary school report cards read, "William should become either a lawyer or an actor because he lies so well." Cosby scored high on intelligence tests, and he was assigned to a high school for gifted students.
30 There, he enjoyed playing football, but his classwork

suffered. He flunked the tenth grade twice, returned to a regular school, flunked again, and finally dropped out. His mother was bitterly disappointed. But even in failure, she says, "Bill was determined to be somebody." That true grit paid off. Cosby completed 35 high school in the Navy and at the end of his four-year hitch won admission to Temple University on an athletic scholarship.

Now, almost every working day, wherever he is in the world, Cosby receives an express-mail packet or a 40 personal courier bearing business documents. Bills for the dentist, for college tuition, groceries—Cosby personally signs checks for all of them. At restaurants and shops he pays cash. Even on purchases like real estate he shuns financing. "For people from a lower 45 economic background," he explains, "it means a lot to know something is paid for."

The Cosby clan owns houses in Manhattan, Philadelphia, and Los Angeles, as well as a 265-acre estate near Amherst, Massachusetts, where the family 50 lives most of the time. There are 22 fine cars at the various homes, including two Rolls-Royces and a 1937 Aston Martin. Cosby also has a seven-passenger Mitsubishi jet.

Cosby's wife Camille has exerted a quiet influence 55 over her husband ever since they met on a blind date in 1963. On the rare occasions when the two are out in public, Cosby treats her with the adoration of a nerdy schoolboy who cannot believe his luck at landing the prom queen. 60

📖 EXERCISE 1: *Meaning from Context*

Match the words in column 1 with the meanings in column 2.

_____ **1.** drive *(line 3)*

_____ **2.** yarns *(line 17)*

_____ **3.** flunk *(line 31)*

_____ **4.** hitch *(line 37)*

_____ **5.** shun *(line 45)*

_____ **6.** clan *(line 48)*

a. stories
b. sum
c. not pass, fail
d. period of time
e. disappointment
f. avoid
g. family
h. determination

DISCUSSION

1. What people do you think the author spoke to in order to get his data?

2. What kinds of records do you think he looked at?

3. What do you think the author saw Cosby do?

4. What do you think the author inferred, based on his knowledge of Cosby?

📖 EXERCISE 2: *The Life of Cosby*

*Read the events in Bill Cosby's life and put them in chronological order. Number them from **1** (first) to **6** (last).*

_____ Cosby flunked tenth grade.

_____ He joined the Navy.

_____ He received $.25 when he told jokes and stories.

_____ He won an athletic scholarship.

_____ He bought an estate near Amherst, Massachusetts.

_____ He scored high on intelligence tests.

Recognizing Subjective and Objective Statements

A biographer gathers facts from interviews with a living subject and other people, and from reading letters, documents, and other records. The writer must decide how to make the story interesting, and not just a list of facts, as well as decide how much of his or her own inferences and imagination to use when facts are not available. The biographer may choose to present a life story objectively (without stating his or her own opinion) or subjectively (including the writer's own or other people's opinions). Recognizing the degree of subjectivity an author has will help you evaluate the credibility and accuracy of the information.

While President, Calvin Coolidge regularly examined his wife's shopping and household bills to see how much money she spent.

This habit shows just how little confidence Coolidge had in his wife's abilities and how he attempted to humiliate and control her at all times.

📖 📖 EXERCISE 3: *Subjective or Objective?*

A. *Read the sentences about Calvin Coolidge in the box. Which of the two statements is objective? subjective? How do you know? Share your ideas with the class.*

B. *Find sentences from the article on Bill Cosby and explain why you think they are subjective or objective to a partner. Then, discuss the author's degree of subjectivity. Did this influence your impression of Bill Cosby? Why or why not?*

WORD FOR WORD!

Compound Words

A compound word, two or more words functioning as one, may be formed with or without hyphenation. A compound word can be a quick way of giving a description, for example, "a month-old baby" instead of "a baby who is a month old." Look back at the article on Bill Cosby and search for compound words with and without hyphenation. How many can you find?

 EXERCISE 4: *Brain-Buster*

Find the compound words in the Cosby article with these meanings and write them on the lines.

1. receiving the most money _____

2. a day laborer _____

3. childhood training _____

4. telling stories _____

5. assignments done in class _____

6. lasting four years _____

7. package sent very quickly _____

8. holding seven passengers _____

 # SPEAK OUT!

Keeping a Conversation Going

In conversation we ask for and exchange information in a number of ways. To keep a conversation going, we use words and expressions that indicate our interest, show our reaction to what is being discussed, and encourage the speaker to continue giving more information. In the conversation, underline the words and expressions that show how Bob and Kim keep their conversation going.

BOB: So what did you do this weekend?

KIM: I had a really great weekend. I did a lot of things I'd never done before!

BOB: Oh really? Like what?

KIM: Well, for one thing, I went to a comedy club and saw a stand-up comic.

BOB: You'd never been to a comedy club before? Why not?

KIM: I don't know, really. I guess I thought it wouldn't be all that much fun to just sit there and listen to someone talk.

BOB: How did you like it?

KIM: I loved the club! I saw a female comic who was so funny I couldn't stop laughing. I mean tears were rolling down my cheeks I was laughing so hard!

BOB: Well who was it? Maybe I'll go to see her myself.

KIM: Her name is Sue Zuki.

BOB: You're kidding! That couldn't be her real name!

KIM: Oh, probably not, but so what? She was so funny!

BOB: Right. So what else did you do that was a first?

KIM: I went rollerblading! Have you ever tried it?

BOB: Are you joking? I love rollerblading! I just got a new pair of rollerblades last weekend.

KIM: What kind did you get? There are so many brands.

BOB: I bought Speed Kings. They're expensive, but the control you get is worth it. What brand do you have?

KIM: Oh, I just rented a pair. But since I had such a good time skating, I think I'll buy some for myself. Where did you get yours?

BOB: At Sport Express over on Seventh Avenue.

EXERCISE 5: *Do Tell!*

Work with a partner. Using topics from the list, take turns beginning conversations. As you speak and listen, use words and expressions to show your interest and reactions. Encourage your partner to keep the conversation going and give more information when possible.

your weekend activities   your last vacation
a frightening moment   a current event
an embarrassing moment   your own idea

FIGURE IT OUT!

Talking About Actions in the Past

There are several ways of talking about the past. Go back to the Cosby article on page 16 and the conversation on pages 18 and 19, and underline all the examples of ways to talk about actions in the past. Identify the tenses used.

EXERCISE 6: *It's All in the Past*

Look at the sentences you underlined and think about what you've learned about the simple past, past progressive, past perfect, and the habitual past. Fill in the chart with the formation of the tense and time words used with each tense.

Simple Past	Past Progressive	Past Perfect	Habitual Past

Write the correct form of the verb on the line.

In addition to his dry sense of humor, Calvin Coolidge was known for being careful with money. He **(1. spend)** _____ as little as possible. When the President of the U.S., Warren G. Harding, **(2. die)** _____ of an illness, his Vice-President, Calvin Coolidge, **(3. sleep)** _____ at his family's summer home in Vermont. Coolidge's father **(4. wake)** _____ him and **(5. tell)** _____ him that Harding **(6. die)** _____. Coolidge **(7. put on)** _____ his pants and **(8. walk)** _____ to the general store with his father, their local Congressman, and a reporter to wait for news from Washington. While they **(9. wait)** _____, Coolidge **(10. ask)** _____ for three soft drinks. When the drinks **(11. come)** _____, the soon-to-be president **(12. pay)** _____ for only one of the drinks he **(13. order)** _____, his own! A short time later, his father, a notary public, **(14. read)** _____ him the oath of office. Coolidge **(15. still/wear)** _____ his pajama shirt. Then both men **(16. return)** _____ home and **(17. go)** _____ back to bed.

📖 **EXERCISE 8:** *Get the Facts!*

A. *Work with a partner. You need the information that your partner has in order to complete a biographical report on a famous cartoonist. Student A will ask Student B questions about Gary Larson, and Student B will ask Student A questions about Cathy Guisewite. Fill in the chart with the information you receive about your cartoonist. Answer your partner's questions by looking at the information on page 21.*

Cartoonist's Name:	
Year born:	Where born:
Feelings about childhood:	
When began to draw:	Hobbies:
Pets:	First sale of cartoons:
Number of newspapers:	Books published:
Themes in work:	

Gary Larson

- born in 1950 in Tacoma, Washington
- "I had a great childhood"; lived in a private world
- began drawing as a child in school
- hobbies include playing guitar and banjo, snake-hunting, basketball
- pet: snakes, including a 150-lb. python
- first work sold in 1975
- cartoons run in more than 900 newspapers
- over fourteen books published
- themes in work include: man is not only species on planet and not the wisest or strongest; people's delight in the misfortune of others; our strange roles and behavior

Cathy Guisewite

- born in 1950 in Dayton, Ohio
- resented her mother's job; hated museums and films
- wrote and illustrated a story at age six
- hobbies include skiing, tennis, going to movies, shopping for bargains
- pet: a dog named Trolley
- first work sold in 1976
- cartoons run in more than 500 newspapers
- over seventeen books published
- themes in work include: struggles of a single career woman; the "four guilt groups of food, love, mother, career," self-improvement and never giving up on problems

B. *Do you enjoy reading the work of cartoonists? Who are some of your favorites? Why do you like their work? Share your ideas with the class.*

C. *Look at the cartoons by Cathy Guisewite and Gary Larson. Do you think they are funny? Why or why not?*

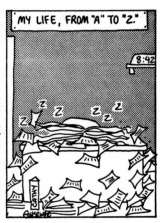

MY LIFE, FROM "A" TO "Z."

"Wouldn't you know it! . . . And always just before a big date!"

"Mr. Osborne, may I be excused? My brain is full."

LISTEN TO THIS!

Who are some of your favorite comedians and comic actors? Why do you like them? Are you familiar with comic personalities from different countries? Who are they?

Mario Moreno   Roseanne Arnold   Peter Sellers

Eddie Murphy   Fernandel   Yakov Smirnoff

 EXERCISE 9: *Cantinflas*

A. *Listen to the episode about Mario Moreno from the program* Radio Biography *and fill in the information in the chart.*

Mario Moreno: Cantinflas
1. when born:
2. where born:
3. amount of first salary earned:
4. date of first appearance at the Folies theater:
5. date of first movies released:
6. date of first social improvement program:

B. *Listen again and then decide if the sentences are true or false. Write* **T** *for true or* **F** *for false on the lines. If the statement is false, correct it. Follow the example.*

_____**F**_____ Mario Moreno grew up in ~~the United States~~.
Mexico City.

1. _____ Moreno decided to change careers after he graduated from agricultural school.

2. _____ After working as a dancer in traveling tent shows, Moreno worked as a touring boxer.

3. _____ Moreno carefully planned the personality his character Cantinflas would have.

4. _____ Cantinflas is from the poor side of town.

5. _____ Cantinflas makes fun of authority, politics, people, and events.

6. _____ After his Hollywood debut, he began to use his money to fight social problems.

7. _____ Moreno is so popular that he is the central figure in a mural painted by the famous Mexican artist Diego Rivera.

8. _____ Moreno has been called Latin America's Charlie Chaplin.

SAY IT CLEARLY!

Past Tense and Past Participle Endings

> People all over the world have laughed at Mario Moreno's hilarious performance as Cantinflas, the confused, pushy but good-hearted simple man of the people. Moreno has succeeded so well that he has founded social organizations and helped many less fortunate people using the money earned from his films and personal appearances.

Work with a partner. Look at the sentences in the box and underline all examples of the different past tense and past participle endings. What are the different pronunciations of the regular endings? When the final sound in the verb itself is /d/ or /t/, how do we pronounce the ending? Compare your ideas with those of your partner.

EXERCISE 10: *The End*

Listen to the conversation and write the regular past tense verb or past participle on the line. Then circle the pronunciation of the ending. There are five examples in the conversation. (See the IPA chart, page 148.)

1. _____   /d/   /t/   /əd/
2. _____   /d/   /t/   /əd/
3. _____   /d/   /t/   /əd/
4. _____   /d/   /t/   /əd/
5. _____   /d/   /t/   /əd/

EXERCISE 11: *Biographical Data*

Work with a partner. Take turns using verbs from the box to ask and answer questions about each other's past. Be careful of your pronunciation of the past tense and past participle endings.

A: What sports did you like to play when you were a child?
B: Well, I **liked** to play tennis, and I **enjoyed** swimming. I **hated** gym class at school, though. What about you?

like	enjoy
hate	help
play	live
move	laugh
cry	paint
join	date
study	vote
work	love

READ ABOUT IT!

Recognizing the Author's Purpose

A. Identifying the author's purpose in writing a text helps reading comprehension. One common purpose authors may have is that of persuasion. What are some other purposes authors commonly have in mind as they write? Make a list.

B. Carol Burnett, one of America's most popular comedians and actresses, tells the following story in her autobiography, *One More Time*. As you read, decide what her purpose was in telling this story. Then share your ideas with the class.

fawn:

Sixth Grade
by Carol Burnett

Mrs. Ernst was my favorite teacher. If our sixth-grade class had been extra-good that week, she'd spend the last hour or so on Fridays reading to us. She was a wonderful actress, and she threw herself into the stories and became all the characters—
5 accents and everything.

I remember when she read *The Yearling* to us. It was the story of a young boy, Jody, who lived in the backwoods of some southern state with his parents a long time ago. It was a story about his love for his pet, a wild fawn named Flag. It was a story
10 about growing up and responsibility, Mrs. Ernst said.

When she got to the part where Flag had to be shot, she "became" Jody, and she started crying real tears and screamed the way a real little kid would. She turned into him right before our eyes.

15 I thought that was a swell thing to be able to do.

I just ate up fairy tales.

All kinds.

When I was in sixth grade at Selma, I illustrated a few of my favorite ones in watercolors, and they were picked by the
20 Hollywood Public Library to represent my class.

My favorite was "The Princess and the Pea" by Hans Christian Andersen. I had drawn the princess trying to get to sleep on top of all those mattresses, with a tiny, wicked-looking pea peeking out from the bottom one. I used a different color and design for
25 each and every one of the mattresses. It took me hours. I emptied the water glass for the brushes dozens of times. Fourteen years later I played that very same princess in a musical on Broadway.

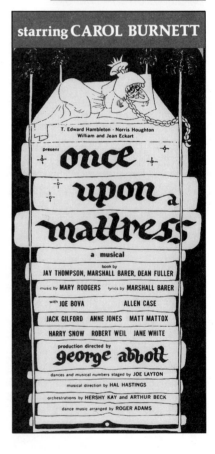

starring **CAROL BURNETT**

once upon a mattress

a musical

EXERCISE 12: *Autobiographies and Biographies*

Work with a partner and answer the questions. Then share your ideas with the class.

1. How are autobiographies and biographies the same? different?
2. Which is probably more objective? subjective?
3. Which requires more research?
4. Which probably contains more inferences?
5. Which is more likely to present the subject in a more positive way?

SPEAK OUT!

Explaining a Decision or Choice

In the reading, you may have concluded that Carol Burnett is talking about some of the events that helped her choose acting as a career. When we explain a choice or a decision, we usually give background information, and we may talk about people or events that have influenced us.

 EXERCISE 13: *It's Your Choice*

A. *Think of an event or a person in your background that has had an important effect on your choice of lifestyle or career. Who or what was it? What decisions have you made because of that person or event? Make notes.*

B. *Work with a partner. Take turns asking and answering questions about his or her event or person. Remember to use the strategies for asking for information, keeping a conversation going, and explaining a decision or choice.*

 WRITE ABOUT IT!

Organizing Your Material

Organizing your material before you begin writing an article or story will help you remember everything you want to say and make your text easier to write. There are many prewriting techniques that can help you organize your ideas. (See the examples on page 26.)

Will Rogers was a U.S. humorist and actor known for his wit. Rogers once made Calvin Coolidge smile, which was reportedly not easy to do. On being introduced to the President, Rogers said, "Now what was that name again?"

Will Rogers

Here are two of the ways Will Rogers' biographical data can be organized:
by **time line** and by **idea map.**

A **time line** organizes information chronologically.

1879 Will Rogers born in Oklahoma
      grew up on father's ranch
      began appearing in cowboy rope-throwing contests
1905 appeared in a cowboy contest in New York
1915 began adding humorous political content to his act
      began writing a humorous political column
      began writing books
1919 published *Rogerisms—the Cowboy Philosopher on Prohibition*
1922 newspaper column syndicated weekly
1926 newspaper column syndicated daily
      began appearing in movies
1931 appeared in *A Connecticut Yankee*
1935 killed in a plane crash in Alaska

An **idea map** organizes material by subject.

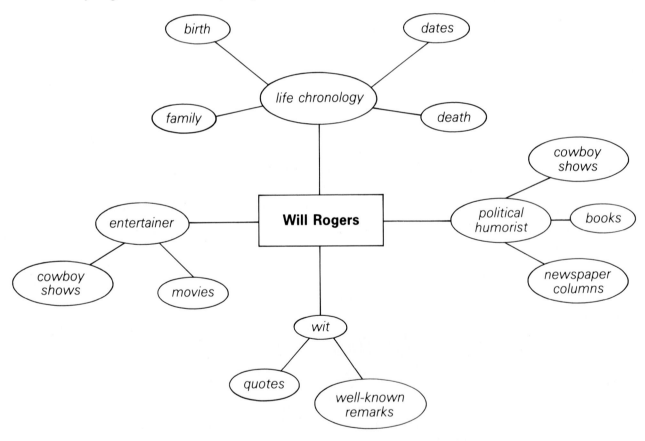

EXERCISE 14: *Organizing Biographical Data*

A. *Imagine you are planning to write a biography. Choose a person you find interesting and then decide what kinds of information you will need in order to write, such as dates, events, personal influences, etc. Develop a time line or idea map with the data you would need.*

B. *Use your time line or idea map to write a paragraph about the person. Follow the writing steps in Unit 1.*

THINK ABOUT IT!

Movie-making is a multi-billion dollar business. People all over the world enjoy going to movies, talking about them, and learning about the lives of movie stars, producers, and directors. Think back to five movies you have seen and enjoyed. What qualities made them special?

TALK IT OVER!

A. Work with a partner. Which character would you like to be in your favorite movie, and why? Would you rather be the director or the screenwriter of that movie? What changes would you have made in the movie?

B. Many different issues, such as youthful rebellion or marriage, are given dramatic treatment in movies. What were the issues in old movies? What are they in current movies? What will the important issues be in future movies? What would they be in your own movies? Share your answers with the class.

READ ABOUT IT!

Using What You Know

What words are associated with the movie business? Think about categories such as jobs, issues, places, and equipment. Brainstorm a list with your class. How will reviewing the vocabulary and ideas you already know help you in preparing to read?

Organizing Information

Good readers know that organizing important information is useful for text comprehension and retention. Scan the article and fill in the chart.

Director	Movie	Year	Issue	Location
Spike Lee	*She's Gotta Have It*	**1.**	relationships	urban
	School Daze	1988	**2.**	**3.**
	4.	1990	race, forced and free choices	**5.**
	Mo' Better Blues	**6.**	African-American life, world of music	urban
	7.	1991	romantic relationships	urban
	Malcolm X	1992	**8.**	
Euzhan Palcy	**9.**		coming-of-age teenagers	Martinique school
	A Dry White Season	1989	**10.**	South Africa
John Waters	**11.**	1988	teen life, nonconformity	small town
	Cry Baby	**12.**	teen life, tolerance	urban

Spike Lee   Euzhan Palcy   John Waters

CLEAR VIEWS FROM THREE VISIONARY FILM MAKERS
by Bea Julian

The eye of a camera captures whatever it is pointing at. For film makers the task is to fuse the images the camera captures into a motion picture that is artistic, interesting, accessible to a wide range of audiences, and generally reflective of something deeper. Making movies—

5 writing, producing, and directing—is not a profession for the faint at heart. Like the most dedicated high-wire artist, it takes daring, courage, skill, technique, and commitment to move in an artistic direction that takes one far above the crowd in search of a better view.

Spike Lee, Euzhan Palcy, and John Waters are three such film

10 makers, unique individualists whose artistic direction has taken them high above the crowd. They each started out as small independents, using their cameras to cut out jarring, but brilliant, viewpoints on life in their separate and contrasting worlds. Their challenging, often controversial films have been perceived by some as garish, flawed, and

15 unrefined, or infinitely fascinating by those who have managed to see them in a different light. They started out in the business young, eagerly translating their styles into independently produced low-budget films that would eventually generate the critical acclaim and audience loyalty needed to tide them over until they achieved the financial

20 success of mainstream Hollywood.

Young New York City film maker Spike Lee relied on both technique and financial savvy to produce in twelve days' time a serious comedy on the subject of personal relationships: *She's Gotta Have It*. A contemporary urban tale of manners and morals,
25 it centers around the affairs of young artist Nola Darling and her three very different boyfriends. The idea of choice introduced in the 1986 film, especially the ways in which we all choose to live together in society, would become a prominent theme in Lee's works. *School Daze*, which followed in 1988, explored the
30 personal choices of students at an all-black college. The idea is explored in even more depth in one of his most controversial films, *Do the Right Thing*, where Lee observes how people work out choices, both free and forced, from the perspectives of residents in an inner-city community in Brooklyn, New York. He
35 guides us through the racial attitudes among cultures that lead to misunderstanding, disharmony, and ultimate ruin—symbolized in the film by the destruction and burning of the pizzeria, a neighborhood tradition. Lee presents what he feels are realistic portrayals of African-American life desperately needed in
40 contemporary motion pictures. This belief is also evident in two subsequent films, *Mo' Better Blues* (1990) and *Jungle Fever* (1991). His next work, a biographical film on the controversial political leader Malcolm X, reflects Lee's conviction that films are a powerful way to stimulate thought, to generate feeling, and to
45 effect change.

Mo' Better Blues

As a child growing up in Martinique, Euzhan Palcy was challenged by her role as an outsider. She developed a love for the movies which was matched only by anger that there were few portrayals of black men, women, and children, and those few were unflattering. Even then Palcy decided that she would use the 50 exciting medium of film to change things. By age seventeen she had written her first script. By age twenty she had acted, written, and directed her first television drama in her native language, French. Film was the right way to open the world's eyes to new visions of the lives of black people living in her home and abroad. 55 One film, *Sugar Cane Alley*, a coming-of-age tale of a young Martinican boy's struggle to gain an education, received major honors and provided international recognition. The artistic success of this film led to Euzhan Palcy's becoming the first black woman to both write and direct a feature film for a major American 60 studio. *A Dry White Season*, a dramatic portrayal of the devastating effects of apartheid in South Africa released in 1989, reflects Palcy's strong belief in the power of cinematic vision to change our way of thinking about the world.

A Dry White Season

65 Yet another way of thinking about our world is represented by the unorthodox visions of Baltimore film maker John Waters. In 1988 Waters produced the commercial hit *Hairspray*, a hilarious portrait of teenage life in the early 1960s rock and roll culture that raised important issues such as non-conformity and racial
70 tolerance. This film was so well received that Waters was able to present a second successful teen portrait, *Cry Baby*, in 1990. In it he again poked fun at those in society who do not let others live their lives in peace.

Even with the changes in audience size and diversity
because of his growing popularity, Waters' beliefs have remained
75 consistent with those of his early days: revelation
through shock, the celebration of personal worth and individuality,
and the need for tolerance.

In fact, when future filmgoers view any of the next Spike Lee,
Euzhan Palcy, or John Waters films, they can expect that the
80 scenes before them on the screen will bear out an artful,
uncompromising, and engaging blend of the eye of the camera
and the film maker's artistic eye. Given these young artists'
energy and vision, film audiences can't help but reach the major
communicative goal that all three film makers share: to make
85 people think.

Hairspray

📖 **EXERCISE 1:** *Meaning from Context*

A. *Match the words in column 1 with the meanings in column 2.*

_____ **1.** unique *(line 10)*

_____ **2.** perceived *(line 14)*

_____ **3.** attitude *(line 35)*

_____ **4.** stimulate *(line 44)*

_____ **5.** unflattering *(line 50)*

_____ **6.** tolerance *(line 80)*

a. encourage
b. produced
c. understanding
d. separate, unusual
e. culture
f. seen, understood
g. negative, unfavorable
h. belief, way of acting

B. *How many of the words from the list you brainstormed earlier
appeared in the article? In what contexts would the other words occur?*

Recognizing Examples and Supporting Statements

When writers develop their main ideas, they strengthen the clarity,
credibility, and authority of those ideas by illustrating them with
examples and supporting statements.

📖 🗣 **EXERCISE 2:** *Read and React*

*Work with a partner or group. Decide to what extent the statements are
true or false and then back up your ideas with examples and supporting
statements from the article.*

1. Film makers do more than record scenes—they interpret them.
2. Lee's, Palcy's, and Waters's movies are a medium for controversial
issues.
3. The movie business sponsors young film makers.
4. Support from critics and audience is very important.
5. It takes a long time to make a serious movie.
6. Spike Lee's films about racism are pessimistic.
7. If you are shocked by a movie, you *think*.
8. The portrayal of minorities in film is usually unrealistic.

WORD FOR WORD!

Talking About Extremes

Statistics indicate that a person has more chance of being a successful brain surgeon than a successful actor. This shows how very hard it is to be a success in the world of movies, but that's show business! In the entertainment field, the vocabulary reflects the extremes of both success and failure.

EXERCISE 3: *Boos and Cheers*

A. *Work with a partner. Match each term from the film world in columns 1 and 2 with its opposite in column 3. Write the letters on the lines. Use a dictionary if necessary.*

_____ **1.** fast-paced   _____ **5.** star   **a.** flop
_____ **2.** controversial   _____ **6.** megabucks epic   **b.** crashingly boring
_____ **3.** film classic   _____ **7.** highly entertaining **c.** low-budget movie
_____ **4.** smash hit   _____ **8.** box office success   **d.** slow-moving
                                                                         e. box office bust
                                                                         f. new release
                                                                         g. extra
                                                                         h. neutral

B. *Use the words to describe some movies you have seen or heard about to your partner. Do you agree or disagree in your opinions?*

> Most people think Charlie Chaplin's movies are film classics, but I find them slow-moving and boring.

Describing Reactions

When we react to movies or other experiences, we often describe our feelings with strongly descriptive adjectives. Many of these terms are noun-verb combinations. For example, we may say that a film that makes us think is a thought-provoking movie.

EXERCISE 4: *How Did You Like It?*

Work with a partner. Look at the movie types in columns 1 and 2 and the descriptions in column 3. Which adjectives would you use to describe each movie type? Write the letters on the lines. Letters can be used more than once.

_____ **1.** horror movie   _____ **6.** war movie   **a.** chair-gripping
_____ **2.** comedy   _____ **7.** science fiction   **b.** nail-biting
_____ **3.** thriller   _____ **8.** musical   **c.** teeth-chattering
_____ **4.** love story   _____ **9.** spy movie   **d.** sidesplitting
_____ **5.** drama   _____ **10.** romantic comedy **e.** gut-wrenching
                                                                     f. heartbreaking
                                                                     g. mind-shattering
                                                                     h. bloodcurdling
                                                                     i. stomach-churning
                                                                     j. foot-tapping

SPEAK OUT!

Encouraging and Discouraging

When we make important decisions, friends, family, and acquaintances give us their opinions of our proposed courses of action. They either encourage us to go on with those actions or discourage us from carrying them out. Look at the words and expressions and classify them as language to encourage or discourage. Write **E** for encourage or **D** for discourage on the line.

_____ Keep at it!

_____ Oh no, whatever for?

_____ That's not a wise course.

_____ I back you up on that.

_____ I don't think you should.

_____ I wish I could too.

_____ I wouldn't if I were you.

_____ You'll enjoy that.

_____ You'll regret it.

_____ It won't work.

_____ I support you on that.

_____ You're way off base.

_____ It's the right thing.

_____ No way!

Anita's family and friends are giving their opinions of her plans. Who is encouraging Anita? Who is discouraging her? How would *you* encourage or discourage her?

A. ANITA: Grandpa's sending me $100 for my birthday next week! Guess what I'm going to do with it! There's an ad in the paper. If I send this acting agency $75, they'll take photos, give me a screen test, and find me a job! The first photo session is on my birthday!

MOM: I really don't think that's a smart idea.

ANITA: Oh, Mom! Why not?

MOM: From what I've heard, these places'll take your money and that'll be the last you'll hear. You'll have wasted your birthday money for nothing.

ANITA: So I'll check them out and find out if they're OK.

MOM: Secondly, you know you'll be graduating in six months, so why not wait?

ANITA: I'm bored with school. I'm going to get a job and make some money.

MOM: It's not easy to find acting jobs. It'll be hard to get any other job without finishing high school. You certainly won't get a good job. It won't work, Anita.

ANITA: I'm going to be an actress, Mom! I'm going to do something with my life.

B. ANITA: Guess what! I'm thinking of contacting that agency about becoming an actress.

GAIL: Fantastic! That's wonderful! I wish I had the money to do that. You're the best actress in our school!

ANITA: Do you really think so? Have I got any chance of success?

GAIL: Of course you have! Just do it! You won't lose anything by trying.

ANITA: I hope you're right. It's what I've always dreamed of doing but never quite dared to try.

GAIL: Go for it! A year from now you'll have made a name for yourself!

And I'd like to thank my friend, Gail, for her support and encouragement.

EXERCISE 5: *If I Were You*

Look at the conversation and underline the words the mother uses to discourage Anita. What are the things she is specifically worried about? How does she express her worries? Share your ideas with a partner.

EXERCISE 6: *Reactions*

Work in groups. First, think of three or four plans or decisions of your own. Write down how you think each member of your group will react to the decisions or plans you've made. Then tell them your plans and check their reactions. Did they encourage or discourage your course of action? Did their reactions surprise you?

FIGURE IT OUT!

Talking About the Future

A. There are many ways to talk about the future. We use the future tenses to talk about future times (calendars, timetables, fixed events), strong intentions, events that are arranged, events that will happen as a matter of course, and events related to conditions. We can use the present progressive to talk about the future, too.

EXERCISE 7: *Back to the Future*

A. *In the conversation, Anita talked about her plans. Underline the verbs in the conversation that refer to the future and write examples of each verb combination on the lines.*

1. will + infinitive _____

2. be + **going to** + infinitive _____

3. present progressive _____

4. simple present _____

5. will + progressive _____

B. *Look at the sentences in column 1 and match them to the correct uses of the future in column 2. Write the letter on the line.*

a. events that are arranged   **d.** events related to conditions
b. events that will happen as a matter of course   **e.** strong intentions
c. timetables, calendars, fixed events

_____ **1.** If Grandpa sends me the money, I'll go to the acting
        agency.

_____ **2.** The picnic'll be on July 4th.

_____ **3.** I'm going to be famous someday!

_____ **4.** I'm having my photos taken at the agency
        at 4:30 P.M..

_____ **5.** The sun will set at 6:42 P.M.

B. Sometimes we choose a point of reference in the future and talk about the time between then and now. When we express our ideas about what will have happened by a certain time in the future, we use the **future perfect tense.**

> By the time I graduate from film school, I will have made my own full-length documentary film.
> The director hopes she will have finished the film by this time next year.
> The writers will have been chosen by next week at the latest.

 EXERCISE 8: *Looking to the Future*

A. *Look at the sentences in the box and identify the elements that make up the future perfect tense. What is the difference between the active and the passive forms?*

B. *List five specific things you will have achieved by the end of this English course. What do you hope you will have learned? Compare your sentences with those of a partner. Do you have similar goals? Do you feel confident you will reach them?*

C. In addition to **will,** we can use other modals, such as **may** or **should** + **have/has** + past participle, to talk about events between now and a future point.

> By the end of the year, we should have made over thirty million dollars with this movie.
> Lee may have won an Oscar by this time next year.

 EXERCISE 9: *By Then*

*Not everyone has the same idea of what the future holds. Work with a partner and make a list of at least five things that you think **will, may, might,** or **should (not)** have happened in the world by the year 2020. Compare your ideas with those of the class. Do you agree? disagree? Do you think these things will have really happened?*

LISTEN TO THIS!

As you know, the film world has a specialized vocabulary. Many colorful and descriptive terms reflect different aspects of the movie industry. For example, the term **spaghetti western** refers to low-budget American-Italian coproductions such as Sergio Leone's *For a Fistful of Dollars* or *The Good, the Bad, and the Ugly* starring Clint Eastwood.

EXERCISE 10: *Movie Report*

A. *Listen to the report from the TV show* Entertainment World *and fill in the chart.*

B. *Listen to the report again and summarize the plot of the film.*

Meeting Venus
1. coproduction:
2. number of languages involved:
3. director's nationality:
4. type of film:
5. number of extras:
6. release date of film:

 SAY IT CLEARLY!

Vowel Lengthening

The sounds /l/, /r/, and /n/ can lengthen the sound of some vowels that precede them. Listen to each pair of words in the box. Which word in each pair has a longer vowel sound? Take turns saying and listening to the words with a partner.

car	care
pin	pan
wall	well
hill	heal

Syllabic Consonants

Most syllables in English words contain a vowel sound. However, /l/ and /n/ can form a syllable at the end of a word that does not contain a vowel sound. Listen to each pair of words in the box. Which word in each pair has a syllable that does not contain a vowel sound?

curtail	cattle
maintain	mountain

EXERCISE 11: *A Fine Ear*

Listen to the passage. Work with a partner. Take turns trying to remember and repeat as much of it as you can. Compare your pronunciation with your partner's, paying special attention to the words with the sounds /l/, /n/, and /r/. Then listen to the passage again to check your work.

 READ ABOUT IT!

At film festivals the world over, filmmakers compete for awards as well as recognition. Festivals are also an opportunity for the general public to see the latest releases. Which towns are famous for their film festivals? Have you ever attended a film festival?

Predicting Organization and Content

An especially useful reading skill is that of predicting what an article will be about. Titles, headings and subheadings, lists, photos, and other graphics tell us much about a text before we read it. The movie review on page 36 is taken from a film festival program. How do you think it will be organized? What will it say?

The Gold Palm Award

1. Why do you think Diego Rivera is described as hard-headed? What other words would describe him?

2. Rivera's wife, Frida Kahlo, is also a well-known artist. What difficulties would two artists working under the same roof have?

3. Imagine you were in charge of making a series of biographical documentaries. Which five famous people would you select as subjects?

DIEGO RIVERA: I PAINT WHAT I SEE
USA

Director:
Mary Lance

Language:
English

Cast:
Julio Mendina
Rosana de Soto
John Hutton
Joe Barrett

Editor:
Sara Fiahko

Music:
Brian Keane

Screenplay:
Eric Breitbart

Cinematographers:
Eric Breitbart
Emiko Omori
Nancy Schreiber
Miguel Ehrenberg

Producers:
Mary Lance
Eric Breitbart

Production
Company:
New Deal Films, Inc.

Print Source:
New Deal Films, Inc.
58 min., 1989

Hard-headed Diego Rivera was the century's most well-known and most brilliant muralist. The title, **Diego Rivera: I Paint What I See,** is taken from a poem by E.B. White, published by *The New Yorker* in the midst of a major controversy, circling around Rivera's mural in Rockefeller Center, which included the face of Lenin. Nelson Rockefeller asked him to remove it but the artist refused. Eventually the mural was destroyed. Using old newsreel shots as well as letters to and from Rivera and his artist-wife Frida Kahlo, the film documents the fame and life of this fascinating Mexican artist. Starting from his childhood in Guanajuato, through his Cubist period in Europe and including his leading role in the Mexican mural renaissance and his fame as a muralist in the U.S. and beyond, we see the growth of an artist as well as the beauty and artistry of his lush designs. Winner of a 1990 CINE Golden Eagle as well as a Special Jury Award at the International Biennial of Films on Art at the Pompidou Center in Paris.

Frida Kahlo and Diego Rivera

SPEAK OUT!

Expressing Contrast and Difference

When expressing an opinion during a discussion, we often use words such as **however, whereas,** and **although** to contrast items and point out differences. In the conversation, how do Yoko and Kent show contrast? Circle the words.

KENT: Even though most people prefer comedies or dramas, I think documentaries are of more value.

YOKO: But they're usually so boring!

KENT: How can you say that? They deal with real life! It's always interesting to find out about real people and real accomplishments. Look at that film about the painter Diego Rivera!

YOKO: Nevertheless, fictional characters and situations have more emotional impact. They seem larger than life!

KENT: Maybe. On the other hand, they don't teach you lessons about real human behavior—everything's made up. Who cares what those people do or how they feel!

 EXERCISE 12: *In Contrast*

Work with a partner. Using words and expressions that show contrast and difference, discuss these questions.

1. What is the value of a film biography over a written one? the value of a book over a film?
2. Which art form is the most/least effective as a medium for treatment of controversial subjects?
3. Predict what you think will have happened to the new movies and directors you discussed earlier in the unit by 2020.

 WRITE ABOUT IT!

Outlines as an Organizing Step

After you have decided on a writing topic, gathered information, and focused, it is helpful to organize your ideas in a systematic way. In Unit 2 you learned about time lines and idea maps. Another useful tool for organizing your ideas in single or multi-paragraph writing is an outline. A **topic outline** orders key words and phrases. A **sentence outline** uses full sentences. Both types use Roman numerals and capital letters to set off the sections. How are other details set off? Look at the outlines about Japan's film maker of genius, Akira Kurosawa, and compare and contrast the two.

Topic Outline

I. Overview of Kurosawa's cultural contribution
    A. As painter and illustrator
    B. As novelist and scriptwriter
    C. As director and producer

II. Biographical data
    A. Birth and family
    B. Childhood
        1. School experiences
        2. Early influences
            a. Brother Heigo
            b. Seiji Tachikawa
    C. Young adulthood
        1. Military school experiences
        2. Art school experiences

III. Influences
    A. Domestic influences
        1. traditional folk tales
        2. books
        3. Kabuki plays
        4. short stories
    B. Foreign influences
        1. Shakespeare
        2. Gorky
        3. Dostoyevsky
        4. John Ford
        5. Jean Renoir

IV. Films
    A. Themes
        1. irony of daily life
        2. personal privacy
        3. dishonesty
        4. corruption
        5. difficulty of knowing "truth"
    B. Cultural impact
        1. controversial subjects
        2. use of color
        3. epic scope
        4. imagination
    C. Influences in others' work
        1. Spielberg
        2. Coppola
        3. Scorsese
        4. De Palma
        5. Japanese directors
    D. Awards and prizes
        1. Silver Lion
        2. Golden Bear
        3. Academy Award
        4. Gold Medal
        5. Mainichi award
        6. order of the Sacred Treasure

Sentence Outline

I. Kurosawa has made a definitive contribution to world culture through his films.
    A. As painter and illustrator, he gained experience that gave artistic impact to his films.
    B. As novelist and scriptwriter, he gained experience in adapting and writing story lines.
    C. As director and producer, he incorporated all his artistic experience to create film masterpieces.

II. Kurosawa's art derives from the stages of his life.
    A. He was born in 1910 into a family of seven children.
    B. Kurosawa's character formed in childhood.
        1. Changing schools as a child influenced Kurosawa's development.
        2. Certain people influenced Kurosawa early in his life.
            a. He looked up to his brother Heigo a great deal.
            b. Seiji Tachikawa encouraged his artistic side.
    C. As a young adult, Kurosawa experimented with different career paths.
        1. He went to military school and studied traditional swordsmanship.
        2. He went to art school and exhibited paintings.

III. Kurosawa was inspired by many different works and important figures in literature and the arts.
    A. Domestic influences include traditional Japanese folk tales, books, Kabuki plays, and short stories.
    B. Foreign influences include the writers Shakespeare, Gorky, Dostoyevsky, and directors John Ford and Jean Renoir.

IV. Kurosawa has an extensive output of quality films.
    A. Themes Kurosawa commonly treats include the ironic treatment of daily life, personal privacy, dishonesty, corruption, and the difficulty of knowing "truth."
    B. Kurosawa's films have had great impact because of his treatments of controversial subjects, his artistic use of color, his epic scope, and his imagination.
    C. Kurosawa's work has influenced many Western film makers, such as Spielberg, Coppola, Scorsese, and De Palma, as well as Japanese directors.
    D. Awards Kurosawa has won include prestigious international prizes such as the Silver Lion from Venice, the Golden Bear from Berlin, the Academy Award from Hollywood, and the Gold Medal from Moscow, as well as many Japanese prizes such as the Mainichi award and the highest-ranking Order of the Sacred Treasure.

 EXERCISE 13: *Your Own Ideas*

Think of several interesting topics related to the world of film. Choose one you like, brainstorm and focus your ideas, and then develop an outline, either topic or sentence, for your subject. Finally, write an article based on the ideas you organized in your outline. Compare your outline and article with those of a partner. Did your article fully develop the ideas in your outline?

THINK ABOUT IT!

How many times in your life have you had to say "good-by" to a person, place, or situation? How did those leave-takings make you feel? Were all of them sad occasions, or were some happy? Were they difficult or easy for you? Think back to two or three of the most important leave-takings in your life. Share your experiences with a partner.

TALK IT OVER!

Do you think the average person in your country moves more or less often than thirty times? How many times have you moved from one home to another? What are the advantages and disadvantages of moving to a new place? Share your ideas with a partner.

> Number of homes the average person lives in over a lifetime: **30**

READ ABOUT IT!

Recognizing the Author's Purpose

Look quickly at the article "Fast-Leaver or Dawdler?" on pages 40 and 41. What do you think the author's purpose in writing the article is? to give advice to the reader on how to say good-by? to help the reader learn something about him/herself? to give information on ways people say good-by? What helped you decide on your answer? Discuss your answer with a partner.

Recognizing and Following Instructions

We as readers interact with the written word in many ways. We can follow a recipe, for example, in order to cook a dish. At other times, we fill out forms to get identification cards and licenses, we answer test questions to pass courses and get jobs, and we do surveys and questionnaires to give and get data. In all of these situations, recognizing and following instructions is an important skill.

Where are instructions generally found? Why is it important to follow instructions? What characteristics do good instructions have? Look over the instructions in the questionnaire. Do you think they are clear? Why or why not? What would you do to make the directions better?

FAST-LEAVER OR DAWDLER?
by Caryl S. Avery

What Your Good-By Timing Says About You—A Test

Every time we move forward, we naturally have to leave something behind. How well we handle this trade-off is crucial to love, intimacy, growth, and success. Some of us are too ready to say good-by to places, people, jobs, even ideas; others are too reluctant. To find out what your leave-taking attitudes reveal about you, take this test.

1. After two years at a great job, you're promoted to another department. You:
   a. skip out early on your last day to avoid a fuss.
   b. feel like a deserter at the send-off party your co-workers throw for you.
   c. plan a weekly lunch with co-workers.

2. You're moving out of your city apartment to a house in the suburbs. You:
   a. busy yourself with packing instead of good-bys.
   b. start to miss the "old neighborhood" even before you've moved.
   c. promise to invite your city friends out as soon as you've settled in.

3. Your parents are moving to a warmer climate to retire. You:
   a. throw a big party for them.
   b. know it's the right thing for them, but can't help feeling abandoned.
   c. plan to visit them in the winter and suggest they come to you in the summer.

4. It's the last day of wilderness-training camp, during which you've become close to your fellow adventurers. You:
   a. say, "so long, it's been great."
   b. feel really down that it's over.
   c. propose a backpacking trip in the fall.

5. Your partner is out of town for a few days on business. You:
   a. view it as time to catch up on things.
   b. feel anxious and lonely, even though he'll/she'll be back soon.
   c. call ahead and have flowers put in his/her hotel room.

6. You've just packed your child off to camp. As the bus pulls away, you:
   a. feel proud of her spunk and pleased at the prospect of a free summer.
   b. look away so she won't see you cry.
   c. wave and hope she writes soon.

ANALYSIS

If your responses were mostly:

a's: Good-bys don't throw you, perhaps because you see a new beginning in every ending—moving becomes moving on—or because you focus on what you had, not what you lost—a wonderful weekend becomes a treasured memory. But if breaking from friends and places **always** comes easily, you may be denying normal feelings of loss. Some people even use frequent leave-taking as a way of avoiding intimacy. Point is, sometimes pangs are appropriate. Those who handle good-bys best tune in to **all** their feelings.

b's: Whether you're the leaver or the left, partings are painful. This means you form deep attachments, but it may also mean you're responding more to past situations than to present ones. Try to recall childhood separations—moving in the middle of a school year or going off to camp for the first time—that could be coloring your adult reactions. While it's natural for some early anxieties to stay with us, keep in mind that you're a different person now, with more resources, coping skills, and resiliency.

c's: Keeping up connections through letters, calls, visits is your way of taking the sting out of separations. Continuity **can** be a source of security when your life is in flux, but you can take this too far. Sometimes you need to cut loose.

EXERCISE 1: *Meaning from Context*

The words in the list appear in the questionnaire. Write the correct form of the word on a sheet of paper.

Henry wasn't enjoying his work. He felt like (1) _____ in the afternoon several days a week, and he got behind in his work and couldn't seem to (2) _____ . When he started really (3) _____ to his feelings, he realized that he wasn't happy at work. He began to think about (4) _____ . He started asking around, and a friend told him about an opening in a small town in the northern part of the state. When he left his city job, he told only his boss to avoid a (5) _____ ; he didn't want a party or a meal at a restaurant. The new place is a (6) _____ ; the job itself is great but the (7) _____ is difficult; winters are terrible. Still, Henry seems to be (8) _____ well. Maybe small town life really suits him.

trade-off
skip out
fuss
settle in
climate
catch up
move on
tune in

EXERCISE 2: *Checking Understanding*

Complete each item in columns 1 and 2 with an item from column 3. Write the correct letter on the line.

_____ **1.** The author says that too many connections to the past mean you may need

_____ **2.** The author has written a quiz

_____ **3.** If you say good-by easily, the author suggests, you may be trying

_____ **4.** If leave-takings are very painful for you, you may need

a. to help you categorize yourself.
b. to understand how your past affects the present.
c. to avoid close relationships.
d. to limit your letters and visits more.

EXERCISE 3: *Parting Shots*

Work in small groups to answer the questions.

1. In the questionnaire you completed, which category did you fall into? Do you think that category accurately describes you? Why or why not? Did you gain any new insights into yourself?
2. Do you think questionnaires of this type are accurate and credible ways to find out more about yourself? Why or why not? What are some other common topics used in questionnaires?
3. This questionnaire deals with aspects of leave-taking. There are many traditional sayings about this topic that reflect different points of view. Read the sayings in the box. Do you agree with them? Do you know of any other sayings that express similar ideas?

> Here today, gone tomorrow. Parting is such sweet sorrow.
> Absence makes the heart grow fonder. Out of sight, out of mind.

WORD FOR WORD!

There are a number of expressions in English made up of a verb and a preposition. These are called two-word verbs. The two words together in each combination usually do not carry the literal meanings of the individual components. The combination has a meaning of its own. Usually, we can figure out the meaning from the context.

> After looking for a present in the mall for two hours,
> Louise **gave up,** left the mall, and went downtown to shop.
> She finally **picked out** a going-away gift for her friend.
> When she got home, she **put** the gift **away** on the top shelf.

Look back at the questionnaire on pages 40 and 41. Underline all the examples of two-word verbs. How many synonyms do you know for those two-word verbs? How many of the two-word verbs do not have the literal meanings of the individual components?

EXERCISE 4: *Out With the Old, In With the New*

Read the paragraph. What do the two-word verbs in dark type mean?
Write the number of each two-word verb on the line next to its meaning.

Cultures all over the world like to say good-by to the old year and welcome the new year with ceremonies, celebrations, and rituals. In some countries, people use the last day of the year to **(1) go over** their past behavior and **(2) make up their minds** about what they want to do differently in the next year. These personal promises to change are called New Year's resolutions. Some people like to **(3) write down** their resolutions; others don't. Some people **(4) speak out** about their resolutions; others **(5) keep** them **in.** And some people really **(6) stick to** their resolutions, while others ignore them and **(7) go on** acting as they always have. Do you make New Year's resolutions? And, more importantly, do you **(8) keep** them **up** as the year goes on?

a. _____ maintain

b. _____ make a note of

c. _____ talk in public

d. _____ don't discuss

e. _____ decide

f. _____ carry out

g. _____ continue

h. _____ examine

SPEAK OUT!

Asking for, Giving, Accepting, and Rejecting Advice

Everyone has problems in life, and we often discuss them with friends and family members. We not only ask for and give advice, we also accept and reject it. In the conversation, underline the expressions Jeanne and Mollie use to give and take advice. Do you think the advice given is useful? Why or why not?

JEANNE: Hey Mollie, can I come in?

MOLLIE: Sure, Jeanne. Please do.

JEANNE: I thought I'd stop by to see how the packing is going.

MOLLIE: Oh, not too bad. I keep on telling myself that unpacking will be a lot easier than packing.

JEANNE: Yeah. I hate putting things in boxes, but I don't mind putting them away in a new apartment.

MOLLIE: Actually, it's not packing that's bothering me. I'm really more worried about settling in a new place. I've lived here since I was born, so I've never had to get used to living somewhere new.

JEANNE: Gee, I'm the opposite. I don't like to stay in one place too long—and I really enjoy getting to know a new city.

MOLLIE: Could you give me some ideas about how to get to know the city? After I unpack, that is!

JEANNE: Actually I'd probably suggest getting out and looking around *before* you finish unpacking. That way you can start feeling comfortable faster. When *I'm* settling in, I love to just get on a bus and go wherever it goes. You can see a lot from a moving bus.

MOLLIE: Oh, I don't know if I could do that. I'd be afraid of getting lost!

JEANNE: It won't be so frightening once you've settled in. But until you feel more at home, maybe you'd prefer to walk—I do that too, all around the neighborhood.

MOLLIE: Walking sounds better.

JEANNE: And I'd start getting a local newspaper right away too.

MOLLIE: I will. And I really appreciate your helping me. You know what I'm going to miss most?

JEANNE: What?

MOLLIE: I'll miss having you come around to give me advice!

EXERCISE 5: *Should I or Shouldn't I?*

A. *Here are some ways people might ask for and give advice. Write down other expressions you know on the lines. Which do you think you might use with your teacher? with your boss? with your neighbor? with a good friend? Share your answers with a partner.*

Asking for Advice
I need some advice.
Help me decide what to do.
I'd really appreciate your
    helping me with a problem I have.

_____

_____

_____

Giving Advice
Have you thought about (complaining)?
You need to (complain).
I would consider (complaining).

_____

_____

_____

B. *There are also a number of ways to accept or reject advice. Which of the following could you use to accept advice? to reject advice? Which are ambiguous (have meanings that are not necessarily clear)? Share your ideas with a partner.*

That's a good idea.
I think I'll try that.
I'm not sure that would help.
Oh, who knows what to do.
That might work for you, but I'm not like you.

I couldn't possibly.
You're right; I will.
I'll think about it.
That might do it.

 EXERCISE 6: *What Should I Do?*

Work with a partner. For each set of roles in the list, think of an appropriate problem to ask and give advice about. Make a conversation for each set of roles in which you take turns asking for, giving, accepting, and rejecting advice.

a doctor and a patient
two cousins
a teacher and a student

a secretary and the boss
two teenagers
a customer and a salesclerk

 FIGURE IT OUT!

A. *Using Gerunds*

As you know, gerunds are a common feature of English. What do you remember about them? Read the conversation and underline all the gerunds.

A:	Saying good-by is hard.
B:	Yes, it is.
A:	I hate saying good-by.
B:	Really? I don't mind saying good-by.
A:	I hate to even think about saying good-by.
B:	Well, I don't exactly *like* to say good-by, but I can do it.
A:	I put off saying good-by as long as I can.
B:	Putting it off doesn't help.
A:	I sometimes try to leave without saying good-by.
B:	Do we have to keep on talking about this?
A:	When I finally manage to say good-by, it's very painful.
B:	I'd like to offer to help, but I have to get back to walking my dog.
A:	Wait! Don't leave without saying good-by!

 EXERCISE 7: *I Knew That!*

A. *What do you know about gerunds? Decide whether the sentences are true or false. Write **T** (true) or **F** (false) on the lines.*

B. *In the conversation, which gerunds act as subjects? as objects?*

_____ **1.** A gerund is the **-ing** form of a verb.
_____ **2.** Gerunds are used as nouns.
_____ **3.** Gerunds cannot follow a preposition.
_____ **4.** Gerunds can follow the main verb in a sentence.
_____ **5.** You can always use a gerund instead of an infinitive (**to** + base verb) after the main verb in a sentence.

B. Gerunds and Infinitives

In English, some main verbs can be followed only by gerunds, others only by infinitives, and still others by *either* gerunds *or* infinitives.

Some verbs followed by **gerunds:**	avoid (can't) help consider dislike	(don't) mind enjoy feel like finish	keep on miss put off suggest

Some verbs followed by **infinitives:**	agree ask choose decide	hope learn manage offer	pretend promise refuse want

Of the verbs that can be followed by either a gerund or an infinitive, some have differences in meaning, while others have no difference in meaning.

I remember **locking** the door.   (I remember that I locked the door.)
I remembered **to lock** the door.   (I had to lock the door and I did.)

Verbs followed by the **gerund** or **infinitive** with differences in meaning:			
forget	regret	remember	try

Verbs followed by the **gerund** or **infinitive** with no differences in meaning:			
begin (can't) stand	continue hate	like love	prefer start

EXERCISE 8: *Here's My Advice*

The author of "Fast-Leaver or Dawdler" divides people into three categories. Work with a partner. Find out which category your partner is in. Take turns giving advice to your partner using gerunds and infinitives.

A: I'm a dawdler for sure. The questionnaire was right!
B: Well then, you may need to stop being so afraid of saying good-by. You should keep in touch, but you could also try looking forward to new experiences and seeing the positive side of change.

C. Time Clauses

Time clauses can be used to say when an event took place or will take place compared to another event. How many words can you think of that express time relationships? Make a list and share it with the class.

In written English, for the sake of brevity, the present or past participle of a verb is sometimes used after a word expressing time, instead of a subject and a verb clause.

 EXERCISE 9: *It's About Time*

Look back at the questionnaire on pages 40 and 41 and conversation on page 43. How many words can you find that express time relationships? Make a list. Compare your list with a partner's.

LISTEN TO THIS!

What are the characteristics of an organized person? Are *you* an organized person? What advice and tips can you give others so that they become organized in their lives? Share ideas in a group.

EXERCISE 10: *Move On Out*

Here are some notes from a seminar titled "Organizing Your Move the Easy Way." They are out of order. Listen to the seminar lecture and number the moving steps in the correct sequence. There are eight steps.

finish personal packing
have car tuned up
notify friends of new address
begin sorting belongings
give movers directions
make final house tour
list people to notify of address change
set up box for important papers

EXERCISE 11: *Moving In*

Work in a small group. Brainstorm a list of the ten most important things to do the day after moving into a new home. Compare your group's list with those of other groups. Do you have the same items on your lists? Which items of all the lists are the most important things to do first? Make a single list of the most important items.

SAY IT CLEARLY!

Variable Stress in Function Words

The stress a word receives may change depending on its position in a sentence. Read the examples in the box.

In the sentences in the box, which of the words in dark type receives stronger stress? What happens to the words with weaker stress? Why do you think so? Share your ideas with a partner. Then listen to the sentences to check your predictions.

> A: What are you looking forward **to?**
> B: I'm looking forward **to** going on vacation next month.
> A: Oh yeah? Where are you planning **to** go?
> B: Hawaii. We're going there because my wife has always wanted **to.**

EXERCISE 12: *Travel Checklist*

Listen to the conversation and decide if the words in the list are stressed or unstressed. Mark an **X** in column 1 for stressed or in column 2 for unstressed.

	stressed	unstressed			stressed	unstressed
1. for	_____	_____	**5.** at		_____	_____
2. for	_____	_____	**6.** at		_____	_____
3. to	_____	_____	**7.** to		_____	_____
4. to	_____	_____	**8.** to		_____	_____

EXERCISE 13: *Look At That!*

Work with a partner. Take turns reading the conversation aloud. Pay special attention to the stress of the words in dark type. When you have finished, listen to the conversation to check your work.

A: Earl, look **to** your right. Can you believe the man in that awful T-shirt?

B: Oh, come on, Thelma, it's no business of ours. He can wear whatever he wants **to.**

A: His wife looks embarrassed. At least she knows why everyone is looking **at** him.

B: Here we are in fabulous Hawaii and a man's T-shirt is all you can look **at?** I don't believe it!

A: Well, what are you getting impatient with me **for?**

B: I'm not impatient, just anxious to go on the tour. I'm here **for** the beautiful scenery.

READ ABOUT IT!

Recognizing Tone

The tone, or attitude, a writer adopts towards the subject and the audience plays an important part in the overall effectiveness of his/her writing. The writer may adopt a playful tone, a serious tone, a sarcastic tone, and so on. In addition, the author must be careful to choose a tone consistent with his/her intent. As you read the article, identify the author's tone.

Bittersweet Memories
by Karen Odom

High school graduation—the bittersweet feelings are as much a part of me now as they were twenty-one years ago.

It was the height of excitement! The months
5 leading up to the big event were packed with special activities—the senior class trip to California and Mexico, rehearsals, not to mention exams, and, of course, the long-awaited senior prom.

As graduation day approached, the excitement
10 only intensified. Being out of high school meant I was finally coming of age! Soon I would be on my own, making my own decisions, doing what I wanted when I wanted without someone looking over my shoulder and it meant going to school
15 with boys—a welcome change coming from an all-girl high school.

There was never any question in my mind that I would go to a coed college away from home. My mother's fantasies, on the other hand, were just
20 the opposite. Trying her best not to force her preferences on me, she would subtly ask whether I had considered particular schools—all of which happened to be located in or near my hometown of Chicago. Once it was established that, as long
25 as it was financially feasible, I would be going away, my family's perspective changed. Their concern shifted from *whether* I was going away to *how far*. The schools I was considering on the East Coast suddenly looked much more appealing
30 than those in California.

But which college I would attend was just one of what seemed like a never-ending list of unknowns: What would college be like? Would I be unbearably lonely not knowing anyone else who
35 was going to the same school? Would the other students like me? Would I make friends easily? Would I miss my family so much that I wouldn't be able to stand it? And what about the work— would I be able to keep up? (Being an A student
40 in high school seemed to offer little assurance I would be able to survive college.) What if the college I selected turned out to be a horrible mistake? Would I be able to transfer to another school?

Then panic set in. My feelings took a 180- 45
degree turn. I really didn't want to leave high school at all, and it was questionable whether I wanted to grow up after all. It had been nice being revered as a senior by the underclass students for the past year; I didn't relish the idea of being on 50 the bottom rung of the status ladder again.

Despite months of anticipation, nothing could have prepared me for the impact of the actual day. As the familiar strains of "Pomp and Circumstance" echoed in the background, I looked 55 around at the other figures in white caps and gowns as we solemnly filed into the auditorium. Tears welled up uncontrollably in my eyes, and I was consumed by a rush of sadness. As if in a daze, I rose from my seat when I heard my name 60 called and slowly crossed the stage to receive my diploma. As I reached out my hand, I knew that I was reaching not just for a piece of paper but for a brand-new life. As exciting as the prospect of a new life seemed, it wasn't easy saying good-by to 65 the old one—the familiar faces, the familiar routine. I would even miss that chemistry class I wasn't particularly fond of and the long commute each day between home and school that I abhorred. Good or bad, it was what I knew. 70

That September, I was fortunate to attend a wonderful university in Providence, Rhode Island. I needn't have worried about liking it. My years there turned out to be some of the best years of my life. And as for friends, some of the friendships 75 I formed there I still treasure today.

Years later, financial difficulties forced my high school to close its doors for good. Although going back is impossible, it's comforting to know I can revisit my special memories any time. 80

EXERCISE 14: *Recognizing the Author's Tone*

A. *What do you think the author's overall tone is in "Bittersweet Memories"? How do you know? What words and details show the author's tone? Discuss your answer with a partner. Do you agree?*

B. *How do you think the tone that was used supports and develops the author's purpose? How does the tone help get across the main ideas? Discuss your answers with the class. Does everyone agree? Why or why not?*

SPEAK OUT!

Expressing Tentative Statements

In conversation, we usually express our ideas in a firm, convincing way, but occasionally we may not be completely sure of what we say, or we may wish to protect ourselves from potential mistakes or inaccuracies. We use words and expressions such as **possibly, I may be wrong but . . . ,** and **I'm not sure of this but . . . .**

In the conversation, underline the words and expressions that show when the speaker is feeling tentative about his/her statements.

BILL:	I may be wrong to be so worried, but I can't help thinking that little Timmy is having trouble with school.
MARY:	Why is that?
BILL:	Well, he cries every morning when I take him to his first-grade class. He grabs me and begs me not to go.
MARY:	Correct me if I'm mistaken, but don't all first graders go through that? Leaving home for the first time, I mean?
BILL:	To some extent, yes, but Timmy's reactions seem to be exaggerated, excessive. At least it looks that way to me. He cries and cries, and sometimes he even throws himself on the floor and kicks and screams.
MARY:	I'm no expert, but it all could mean that he just isn't ready for separation from his parents.
BILL:	But he went to preschool last year and had no big problems adjusting then. I could be off base here, but I think it's more than not wanting to say good-by.

 **EXERCISE 15:** *Possibly*

*Look back at the types of leave-takers on page 41. Which category of leave-taker, type **a, b,** or **c,** do you think the writer of "Bittersweet Memories" falls into? Why? Work with a partner. Discuss your decision. Are you sure of your answer? If not, use the language for expressing tentative statements in your conversation.*

EXERCISE 16: *It Could Be That. . . .*

"Bittersweet Memories" deals with one student's memories of high school and college. A number of students have a difficult time adjusting to a new school environment. Why is school such a stressful and sometimes painful experience for some students? Work in small groups to brainstorm ten possible reasons. Include reasons you can firmly support and others you feel tentative about. Introduce those ideas to your group using the appropriate language.

WRITE ABOUT IT!

Cubing

A. As you know, a cube is a geometric shape with six equal sides. We can use this organizing principal of six sides as a prewriting step. When using cubing, writers make notes about six different sides or aspects of their subject as a way to begin writing and develop their ideas. The six approaches in cubing are:

B. Here is one writer's use of cubing as an approach to writing about coming home unannounced after a long absence.

Describing: What does the subject to be treated look like? What size is it? color? shape? texture? How many parts does it have?

Comparing: What is the subject similar to? different from?

Associating: What does it bring to mind? What connections does it have to anything else in the writer's experience?

Analyzing: How is it made? Where did it come from? Where is it going?

Applying: What can be done with it? What uses does it have?

Arguing: What arguments can be made for it? against it?

Describing: December, just before New Year's Eve; coming from overseas; hadn't seen family in 2 years; didn't phone first; wanted to surprise them

Comparing: emotional reactions different from coming home other times; had been gone much longer; similar to other homecomings because of warm welcome

Associating: memories of an uncle returning from war; a sister visiting after settling in another country; powerful emotions; movies about happy and sad homecomings; reasons for homecomings: voluntary absence; war; getting lost; hospitalization; prisoners

Analyzing: why homecoming was a surprise; how arrangements were made to keep it a surprise; results of surprise

Applying: apply to making decisions about being absent and coming home in the future; how will it feel to be the parent someday; emotions of homecoming as a way to make family stronger

Arguing: argue for strong feeling of anticipation for homecomer; no fuss for family; argue against family being deprived of feelings of anticipation and opportunity to make a fuss

EXERCISE 17: *Cube It!*

Work in small groups. Work together to develop an article on moving away from home for the first time. Keeping the topic in mind, spend three to five minutes developing each side of the cube. Begin with what you know about the subject, but also make notes to get more necessary information when needed. When you have finished with all six sides, compare your ideas with those of another group. Did you develop all of the sides equally? Did you organize your material in similar ways? Did all your ideas relate to your topic?

EXERCISE 18: *On Your Own*

Use cubing to organize your ideas and write about one of the following topics:

moving away from home for the first time
starting a new job
saying good-by to a dear friend who is moving overseas

THINK ABOUT IT!

When you ask people what they do for a living, most people will give you answers you recognize; for example, teacher, mechanic, office worker, sales clerk, dentist. But some people have more unusual jobs: chimney sweep, advice columnist, skydiving instructor. Think about people you have met or heard about. Did any of them have unusual jobs? What were they? Share your list with the class.

skydiver   *chimney sweeps*

TALK IT OVER!

Look at the cartoon. What do you think the man's job is? What do you think happened to him? What are some other jobs that involve exposure to danger or accidents? Share your ideas with a partner.

READ ABOUT IT!

Getting Information from the Newspaper

Newspaper articles are often accompanied by photos, graphs, diagrams, or charts. Large and small headlines call your attention to the article. Captions under photos and other graphics identify the graphics and relate them to the article.

ELEPHANT HOUSE

"They've decided it *was* a job-related accident."

What attracts your attention and makes you want to read a newspaper article? the size of the headlines? photos? the subject? the writer's name? Discuss your answers with the class.

EXERCISE 1: *Predicting from Pictures and Headlines*

Look at the headlines and the photos for the article on pages 52 and 53. On a sheet of paper, write three things that you think this article will be about. Share your ideas with the class.

Making Inferences

Writers often provide information in an article without actually stating it. The reader gets this information by **making inferences**, or by "reading between the lines." As you read the newspaper article, notice places where the writer expects you to figure out information that is not stated directly.

A Bang-Up Job
by William Ecenbarger

Mr. Fireworks, George Zambelli, is heir to an explosive
tradition that dates from ancient times

They are costly, risky and unpredictable, with lifetimes no longer than
the length of their fuses. They were a diversion of European monarchs,
yet the Founding Fathers adopted them to celebrate independence from
King George III. They have caused more casualties than the entire Rev-
5 olutionary War: More Americans have died celebrating their independence than achieving it.

Although most states now restrict the use of fireworks by individuals,
there remains a small band of skilled pyrotechnicians to put color and
sound in the sky on the 4th of July. They are nearly all descendants of
10 Italian immigrants who brought their skill with them. They consider
themselves artists—painters whose canvas is the night sky.

The loftiest of this group is The Great Zambelli. Or, as a news release
once put it, ''Mr. Fireworks, George 'Boom Boom' Zambelli, the inter-
nationally renowned pyrotechnic king, President of Zambelli Interna-
15 tionale Fireworks Manufacturing Co. Inc.''

Zambelli Internationale was founded by his father, Antonio, near
Naples in 1900, and he brought the business to New Castle, Pennsylva-
nia, in 1920. George began rolling firecracker tubes at age 7, and by 16
he was a shooter.

20 Other Italian pyrotechnicians came here at the same time, and during
the '30s, 25 percent of all American fireworks were produced in New
Castle.

''Fireworks has always been a family business,'' Zambelli says.
''Hey, it's a dangerous business, and you have to trust the person work-
25 ing next to you. That's why we keep it in the family, OK?''

Each family business has its own formulas for various types of fireworks, called recipes, that are guarded as closely as those for Coca-Cola
and Col. Sanders' chicken. The Zambelli recipes were written down in
Italian in a little black book, carried across the Atlantic and now repose
30 in a safe in Z Penn Centre.

The basic ingredients are potassium nitrate, sulfur and charcoal (creating gunpowder), which when combined with other chemicals are transformed into colored lights moving in controlled patterns.

35 Zambelli Internationale makes its fireworks at an isolated 360-acre site about 10 miles from the Ohio River. From the air, it looks like a miniature golf course: tiny groups of structures widely spaced out and connected by worn paths. These concentrations 40 are concrete-block buildings, each about the size of a one-car garage. They are called magazines, and each produces a different type of firework. There are 22 magazines in all. When a magazine door is opened, the smell of black pow- 45 der leaps out. Two or three aproned workers labor in each magazine.

Although death is but a spark away, the work- 50 ers seemed uncon- cerned, floating along the current of the day as though this were a gar- ment factory. A young 55 woman sits at a wooden treadle, pulling string around a cardboard can- ister loaded with explo- sives.

60 Display fireworks are packed either in a tube

Aerial view of Zambelli magazines

about the size of a tennis ball can or a round shell about the size of a bowling ball. The pyrotechnician decides what the firework should do and packs the 65 shell accordingly. The way the shell is fused, the arrangements of the ''stars''—chemical pellets that produce the colors—and the arrangement of the ''sa-

lutes''—the stuff that gives the bangs—are responsi- ble for the effect of the firework.

The shell is placed in a long tube called a mortar. 70 Black powder packed at the bottom of the shell is ignited, and expanding gas propels the shell out of the mortar. The stars, about the size of sugar cubes, determine the colors. White is difficult to produce, but a display with blue has the master's touch. The 75 blue flame is one of the most difficult because it re- quires copper chloride, which will emit blue light only when the star heats up to 1,000 degrees—and if the star burns any hotter than that, the flame will turn red or green. 80

There is virtually no ma- chinery in the manufac- turing process because of the danger that it will cause an explo- 85 sion. Static electricity is a constant threat, and Zambelli employees are cautioned not to comb their hair at work, and 90 they are not allowed to wear synthetic clothing that could cause a lethal spark.

There have been two 95 serious explosions at Zambelli Internationale. Zambelli's brother-in- law was killed in a 1950 blast, and in 1976 two workers were injured in an explosion. By industry 100 standards, this is a remarkable safety record. Fire- works plants have long been among the world's most dangerous workplaces.

from the Chicago Tribune

📖 **EXERCISE 2**: *Meaning from Context*

Match the words in column 1 with the meanings in column 2. Write the letter on the line.

_____ **1.** casualties *(line 4)*	**a.** designs
_____ **2.** renowned *(line 14)*	**b.** authority
_____ **3.** closely *(line 27)*	**c.** parts, items
_____ **4.** ingredients *(line 31)*	**d.** become
_____ **5.** patterns *(line 34)*	**e.** deaths
_____ **6.** turn *(line 79)*	**f.** habits
	g. famous
	h. carefully
	i. skills

📖 **EXERCISE 3:** *Suffixes of Agent*

A. *As you know, many job names often end with a suffix of agent such as **-er, -or, -ess, -ist,** or **-ian.** Go back to the article and see how many agents you can identify. (There are at least five. Remember, an agent can also be a thing.) When you have finished, compare your words with those of a partner.*

B. *Among the words you found, which are more common? more recognizable? more general? more specific? Make a word map that shows how the words relate to one another.*

👤📖 **EXERCISE 4:** *Making Inferences*

A. *Read each sentence and decide if the information is a fact stated in the article or an inference drawn from it. Circle **F** for fact or **I** for inference. Then discuss with a partner how you decided whether each statement was a fact or an inference. Point out the information you used from the text.*

1.	**F** **I**	A pyrotechnician makes and sets off fireworks.
2.	**F** **I**	The writer of the article visited the Zambelli Internationale factory.
3.	**F** **I**	Red and green are easier to produce than blue.
4.	**F** **I**	Zambelli workers do not have neatly combed hair at work.
5.	**F** **I**	Repair bills for machinery are very low at the Zambelli factory.

B. *Look at the text again and write three inferences of your own on a sheet of paper. Then have a partner find the sections of the text that support the inferences you have made.*

WORD FOR WORD!

Compound Words Describing Jobs

The names of many occupations are compound nouns. As you learned in Unit 2, you can often figure out the meaning of a compound word by looking at the meanings of the smaller words which form the compound. With some compounds, however, you will need to use a dictionary, because the parts come from older words which are no longer used except in compounds.

> songwriter: one who composes songs   (words still in use)
> fishmonger: one who sells fish   **(monger** from the 14th century)

👤👥 **EXERCISE 5:** *Wordwise*

A. *Work with a partner. Read the list of compound job names and answer the questions.*

locksmith	blacksmith	silversmith	glassblower	paymaster	ballplayer
cowboy	welldigger	turnkey	carhop	stagehand	homemaker
cowgirl	wheelwright	playwright	doorman	ringmaster	copywriter
handyman	housekeeper	gamekeeper	weatherman	lamplighter	petsitter
watchman	beekeeper	timekeeper	innkeeper	cowhand	bellhop
gatekeeper	zookeeper	bookkeeper	headmistress	househusband	babysitter

1. Which word endings probably mean **person in charge of?**
2. Which word endings probably mean **creator?**
3. Which word endings probably mean **person who maintains?**
4. Which parts of the compounds are words that are no longer in use? How can you tell?

B. *Take turns describing the meaning of the words in the list.*

Comparisons

To make the description of an unfamiliar object clearer, we can compare the unfamiliar object to a familiar one.

> Fireworks are made in concrete buildings, each **about the size of a garage.**

 EXERCISE 6: *Comparisons*

A. *Scan the article on pages 52 and 53 for comparisons. Write a list on a sheet of paper.*

B. *Work with a partner. Take turns describing the objects in the picture.*

 SPEAK OUT!

Justifying a Choice

Often we are asked to explain why we have made a certain choice or carried out a particular action. We then give reasons and plausible explanations justifying our decision or behavior.

Describing a Process

When we describe a process, we talk about how a procedure happens or how something is done or made. The process may occur in nature or may be something humans or animals do. In describing a man-made process, which do you think is usually more important, the person or thing doing the action, or the action itself?

ANNE: I was told you have a very odd job. What did you say you do?

RICH: I'm a bicycle cameraman.

ANNE: Ah, so you take pictures of bicycles!

RICH: Well, no, not exactly. Actually I use a camera on a bicycle to do filming for movies and commercials.

ANNE: Oh, I see. You ride a bicycle and hold a movie camera at the same time. Do you work for a circus, then?

RICH: No, but, like the circus, the work I do is interesting and always varied. I don't like the same routine every day. I expect most people feel the same way.

ANNE: But do you get satisfaction from such an odd job? And can you make a living from it?

RICH: Of course I make a living from it! It's not the best-paying job, but then money isn't the most important thing to me. I like the variety and the creativity involved!

ANNE: So tell me more. Don't you get tired of riding around on a bike holding a camera?

RICH: Actually, the camera is attached to the bicycle, so I ride using both hands.

UNIT 5 ODD JOBS

ANNE: So how does the camera work?

RICH: Well, after the camera has been mounted on the bicycle—it's not that difficult—the film is loaded, then the camera's connected to the power, and then I start riding along behind whatever the director wants to film.

ANNE: Does this camera get plugged in somewhere?

RICH: I wear a battery pack around my waist, actually.

ANNE: And then you just start filming?

RICH: Not really. There's a button on the bicycle's handlebars I can push when I want to film.

ANNE: I don't want to sound insulting, but why would anybody want to use film that's been taken with a bicycle-mounted camera? It seems like kind of a one-time thing.

RICH: Well, the camera can be mounted only two or three inches from the ground, so you get a very realistic view of, say, someone being chased, or of a race, or of an animal running. And I can get really close to the edge of a cliff, or go between two racing cars, or between trees in a forest. It's pretty effective-looking on the movie screen.

ANNE: Huh. I guess that *would* look good in a movie. Whatever made you get started doing something like this?

RICH: Well, I had done a lot of bicycle racing, and I got interested in filming, so it seemed like a good thing to try. I'm glad I did.

ANNE: But how did you get a *job* doing it?

RICH: Oh, that part was easy. The bicycle-mounted camera job was offered to me by my uncle—he's a film director!

EXERCISE 7: *Because I Want To!*

A. *What choice does Anne ask Rich to justify? How does Rich respond? Why do you think Anne asks him to explain his decision? Underline the sentences in which Rich justifies his choice. Compare your answers with those of a partner.*

B. *Work with a partner. Look back at the list of jobs on page 54. Take turns choosing one of the more unusual jobs and justifying that choice as your lifetime work.*

EXERCISE 8: *It Works Like This*

A. *What process did Rich describe in the conversation? Think about the ways to organize information you have studied. What kind of order did Rich use? What words signal the order Rich used?*

B. *Look back at the reading on page 52. What process does the article describe? Discuss your answer with a partner.*

C. *Imagine that you have one of the jobs in the list on page 54. (Or think about your present job or a job you'd like to have.) Describe a process related to your job to a partner.*

FIGURE IT OUT!

A. *The Passive Voice*

As you know, we often describe procedures and processes in the passive voice. We use the passive when it is important to focus on the process rather than the agent (the doer of the action), when the agent is unknown, or when the agent is generally understood.

> Until recently, most liquids, such as milk and pop, were sold in reusable glass bottles, but today, plastic bottles are much more common because they are cheap and easy to make. Many people are involved in making a plastic bottle. First, a mold has to be designed by an engineer. Then, the mold is made by a mold-maker. Next, the mold is put onto a molding machine by a set-up worker. The machine is loaded with plastic pellets about the size of small peas. The mold is closed, and the plastic is melted and forced into the mold, where it is cooled until it is hard. Then the mold is opened and the bottle is pushed out. Then the mold is closed again, and the process is repeated. While the machine is molding, excess plastic is removed from the bottle by a worker. The finished bottles are packed in boxes.

 EXERCISE 9: *I Remember That!*

A. *Underline all of the examples of the passive voice in the paragraph on plastic bottles. Compare your answers with those of a partner.*

B. *Review what you know about the passive voice by answering the questions. Circle the letter.*

1. We form the passive voice with a form of the verb **to be** plus
   a. an infinitive.   **b.** a past participle.

2. When the agent is mentioned in a passive sentence, it is usually preceded by the preposition
   a. of.   **b.** by.

EXERCISE 10: *Bottles*

Write the correct form of the verb in the passive voice on the line.

After the bottles **(1. make)** _____ , they

(2. send) _____ to a bottling factory. At the factory, the

bottles **(3. put)** _____ onto a bottling machine. They

(4. fill) _____ with liquid, such as milk, and then they

(5. close) _____ and **(6. put)** _____ into

boxes. The boxes **(7. send)** _____ to stores.

B. *Passive Forms with Other Tenses and Modals*

The present perfect, the past perfect, the future, and the future perfect tenses can be used in the passive voice. The progressive forms of these tenses are rarely used in the passive. Modal verbs such as **will, would, should, can, may, might,** and **had better** can also be used in passive voice constructions.

Active Voice

Exploding fireworks **have injured** many people.
By 1951, an explosion **had killed** Zambelli's brother-in-law.
Many states **will pass** laws on fireworks safety in the near future.
Five years from now these laws **will have reduced** accidents.
A spark from static electricity **can cause** an explosion.

Passive Voice

Many people **have been injured** by exploding fireworks.
By 1951, Zambelli's brother-in-law **had been killed** by an explosion.
Laws on fireworks safety **will be passed** in the near future.
Five years from now accidents **will have been reduced**.
An explosion **can be caused** by a spark from static electricity.

EXERCISE 11: *Recyclers*

Decide if the verb should be active or passive. Write the correct form of the verb on a sheet of paper.

Did you know that plastics **(1. can/recycle)** _____ ? In the last few years, many recycling centers **(2. open)** _____ to gather old plastic bottles, and a number of plants **(3. build)** _____ to recycle the bottles. Many people now work in recycling.

In order for plastic to be recycled, recyclers (workers who recycle) must complete several steps. First, plastic **(4. must/bring)** _____ to the recycling center by the public. Then, the recyclers **(5. must/sort)** _____ the plastic by type. Then the plastic **(6. send)** _____ to the recycling plant, where workers **(7. make)** _____ it into new products.

Recycled plastic has many advantages. It **(8. can/use)** _____ for many purposes, such as insulation, packaging, and even "plastic wood" for parks and playgrounds. Recycled plastic **(9. cost)** _____ less than new plastic too. Also, towns are cleaner because of recycling. Recently, ten "plastic wood" benches **(10. donate)** _____ to two Florida communities by a large recycling company. The benches **(11. make)** _____ from trash which **(12. find)** _____ on Florida beaches. Now beachwalkers will be able to **(13. use)** _____ that trash—again and again.

Because of the advantages, some communities **(14. require)** _____ their citizens to recycle various materials. And nonrecyclable plastic **(15. ban)** _____ in some places.

Bench made from recycled plastic

LISTEN TO THIS!

Fireworks are an important part of celebrations around the world. What do you know about the origin and history of fireworks? Share your knowledge with the class.

 EXERCISE 12: *The Gist of It*

A. *Listen to the news report. Which statement best sums up the gist, or main idea, of the news report? Circle the number.*

1. Fireworks have been used to celebrate important events for hundreds of years.
2. Fireworks were invented in China, and then brought to Europe much later.
3. The first fireworks didn't produce displays of lights; over time, color has been added.
4. Fireworks have always been especially important to kings and queens and their celebrations.

B. *Justify your answer for **A** to a partner.*

 EXERCISE 13: *Details, Details!*

Now find out some details. Read the questions. Then listen to the report again to find the answers to the questions. Write your answers on a sheet of paper.

1. Who invented fireworks?
2. When is the first recorded instance of the use of firecrackers in China?
3. When did Roger Bacon find the recipe for gunpowder?
4. When were fireworks brought to Europe?
5. Who brought fireworks to Europe?
6. When were colors introduced into fireworks?

 SAY IT CLEARLY!

Stress Patterns in Compounds

Compound adjectives and nouns, whether they are noun + noun, noun + adjective, or other combinations, have a regular stress pattern. Syllables in each part of the compound receive stress, but the stressed syllable in the first part receives stronger stress and the stressed syllable in the second part receives a slightly weaker stress. Other nouns following these compounds in the phrase also receive main stress.

a forty-acre farm in the foothills   a month-old baby with beautiful eyes

EXERCISE 14: *Predicting Stress*

A. *Predict the stress pattern of each compound word in the sentences. Double underline the syllables with primary stress. Underline the syllables with secondary stress.*

1. A seven-passenger jet landed on the runway.

2. Fourth-of-July fireworks are a popular tradition in the U.S.

3. I found the professor's well-written article very informative.

4. This diagram explains how shell-type fireworks are made.

B. *Listen to the sentences and check your predictions.*

EXERCISE 15: *Stress Patterns*

A. *Read the conversation and mark the stress of the compound words in the dialogue. Double underline the syllables with primary stress. Underline the syllables with secondary stress.*

A: I know the teacher means well, but I think she gives us too much homework! Carrying all these books is a back-breaking task!

B: I know what you mean. Does she think hard-living teenagers like us don't have better things to do? Like going to parties?

A: Well, she believes in old-fashioned values like hard work, I guess.

B. *Work with a partner. Compare your answers in* **A.** *Then say the dialogue aloud. Pay special attention to the stress of the compound words. Then change roles and say it aloud again.*

 READ ABOUT IT!

Diagrams and Charts

Diagrams and charts are often used to illustrate magazine and newspaper articles. You can use diagrams and charts to help you figure out new vocabulary, understand how something is made or works, and form an idea of what the article is about.

 EXERCISE 16: *The Big Bang*

A. *Look at the diagram explaining how shell-type fireworks are made and then put into place at a fireworks display. Notice how the drawings clarify the specialized vocabulary and the sequence of the steps.*

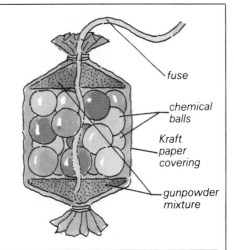

Shell-type firecracker

Shell-type fireworks are made of condensed, powdered chemicals wrapped in thick, cylindrical paper tubes. The tubes are glued together and secured at each end. A strand of threads called a *fuse* ignites the gunpowder, setting off a charge at the bottom of the shell. This charge causes the explosive to shoot into the sky. Once launched, the explosive shoots brightly colored sparks in all directions. Spectacular effects can be made with fuses set to go off at different intervals, or by fireworks that combine mixtures of different chemicals.

fuse

chemical balls

Kraft paper covering

gunpowder mixture

Chemical Colors	
sodium salts	deep yellow
calcium	red
strontium	deep red
barium	green
copper	blue, green
magnesium, aluminum	bright white

B. *Using the information in the diagram, write sentences explaining the process of making and setting up shell-type fireworks. Order your sentences in sequence and use the passive voice when appropriate.*

SPEAK OUT!

Voicing a Complaint and Insisting

Often we have strong feelings about a product, event, or situation. To express dissatisfaction politely but firmly, we first state what the problem is and include details and examples to strengthen our position. Finally, we state what we would like to see done about the problem. If the person we are complaining to does not agree, we have to insist—state our wish more strongly.

Rich, the bicycle cameraman, just bought a new bicycle, but he's not satisfied.

A: Customer Service Department, Murphy Bicycle Company.

B: Hello. I have a complaint to make about a bicycle that I bought by mail.

A: What seems to be the problem?

B: Well, I bought a very expensive Road Master Bicycle, but I found several things wrong with it. First of all, the directions for putting it together were very unclear and even contradictory. Also, the color of the paint on different parts was not the same. Then, when I got it together, it would not ride. I took it to a bike shop, and they told me that they couldn't fix it. They also said that your company's bikes aren't very strong, anyway.

A: I'm sorry to hear that you feel dissatisfied. The Road Master is a very popular bike.

B: Well, I'm a bicycle cameraman. I need a bike that's strong enough to hold my camera. I'd like my money back!

A: It's not a company policy to refund money, but if you mail the bike back to us, we can send you a different bike.

A: Well, I really don't want another bike since the bike shop says that your bikes are not very good. I insist on getting my money back. Let me speak to the head of your department.

B: I'll see if she's available now. One moment, please.

EXERCISE 17: *Customer Dissatisfaction*

Work with a partner. Take turns complaining about the quality, performance, or price of the products in the list. Be polite, but firmly express your dissatisfaction.

1. a transistor radio
2. a package of cheese
3. a computer

4. a diet soft drink
5. a game
6. your own idea

 WRITE ABOUT IT!

Organizing Your Writing

As you know, a good paragraph includes: a **topic sentence** that gives the main idea of the paragraph, **supporting sentences** that give details about the topic of the paragraph, and a **concluding sentence** that brings together the ideas contained in the paragraph. Whether your intention is to complain, inform, or describe, your paragraphs will be more effective when they follow this pattern.

 EXERCISE 18: *Describing an Event*

Think back to a fireworks display, a concert, a play, or some other activity that you enjoyed attending. Brainstorm and focus your ideas, and then write a paragraph describing that event. Be sure to include a good topic sentence, supporting sentences, and a concluding sentence. When you have finished, show your work to a partner to discuss content, clarity, and organization.

 EXERCISE 19: *Writing About a Process*

A. Do you know how newspapers are printed? how pickles are made? how photographs are developed? how paper is made? how walls are papered? how coffee is made? Work with a partner. Decide what elements would be important to include in a description of one of these processes. How would you order the steps? What language structures would be appropriate?

B. Imagine that you have one of the professions in the list. Write a description of a process related to the profession. Remember to develop a good topic sentence, include steps of the process in sequence, and write a concluding sentence. When you have finished, show your work to a partner to discuss content, clarity, and organization.

1. a newspaper recycler in a recycling center
2. a food tester in a frozen food factory
3. a mechanic in a garage
4. an underwater photographer for a nature magazine
5. a computer operator in a large company
6. an idea of your own

THINK ABOUT IT!

A. Specific foods have different associations for different people. For example, many people associate cake with friends, celebrations, and happiness. What do you associate with each of the foods in the pictures? Write one or two associations for each food on a sheet of paper. Compare your associations with those of a partner. Are they the same? different?

a hamburger
spaghetti with meatballs
salad
vegetable stew
coffee and coffeecake
rice

B. What foods do you eat when you're tired? at a celebration? Fill in the chart.

Occasion	Foods You Eat
When you're tired	
When you're happy	
When you're sick	
When you're nervous	
When you're at a celebration	

TALK IT OVER!

A. Where do you buy your food? Why? Why do you choose one place instead of another? Is one better than another? What advantages and disadvantages does each one have?

B. What kinds of food do you associate with each place? What other things do you associate with each one? what sights? what smells? what tastes? Share your answers with the class.

READ ABOUT IT!

Making Predictions from a Title

As you know, we can get ready to read by
using the title of an article to anticipate the kind
of information we will find in the article. Read
the title of this article. Then make a list of five
different foods or drinks and the reasons we eat
them.

> People eat chocolate because it lowers stress.
> People drink cold drinks in summer to cool off.
> People in coastal towns eat a lot of seafood
> because it's usually cheap and plentiful.

Using Parts of Speech to Figure Out Meaning

Many words can function as more than one part of speech, such
as nouns and verbs. We can use our knowledge of parts of
speech to figure out the exact meaning of each use of the word.
For example, in the sentence in the box, which part of speech is
warm, adjective or verb? What does **warm** mean as an
adjective? as a verb? As you read the article, note the part of
speech of **roast, fry, candy,** and **spice.**

> In winter, hot foods are served to **warm** people.

Why We Eat What We Eat
by Karen Odom

Candied grasshoppers or fried termites are considered to be
mouth-watering, lip-smacking treats to eat in China and parts of
west Africa, just as roasted mice and caterpillars are scrumptious
edibles in parts of southern Africa. Most North Americans,
5 however, would be surprised if they were offered any of these as
food and probably wouldn't want to try them. Similarly, Americans
may say that they are "hungry enough to eat a horse," but if
they were in Argentina or France, they would never dig in and eat
the horse meat served in various regions of these countries.

10   What makes us choose the foods we do, and what makes
certain foods desirable in one country but not in another? The
experts do not have a single answer to this question, but rather
several. Actually, what motivates us to choose certain foods over
others is a complex blend of several factors—the foods we have
15 been exposed to during our childhoods, the geography of our
countries, the associations we make with specific foods used in
celebrations and feasts, and our countries' individual customs and
traditions. In fact, the choices we make about food often have
less to do with nutrition than with customs and pleasure.

20   Consuming foods for pleasure can be traced back to when we
were fed milk as infants—our first experience in associating food
with comfort, human contact, and enjoyment. Later in our lives,
without even realizing it, we may reach for the same foods that
gave us comfort in the past, such as chicken soup, which we
25 were served when we were sick; ice cream, which we were
given as a special treat or reward; or chocolate, which we
received on birthdays or Valentine's Day. We associate these
foods with being loved, and they bring comfort in times of stress.

termites:

caterpillars:

The particular foods that people find comforting vary from
30 culture to culture, as do the foods used during celebrations and
feasts. Generally, colder countries have traditionally served hot
foods to warm up people who have to travel in the cold, while
countries with warmer climates are accustomed to serving cold
foods to keep cool. For example, North Americans eat a dinner of
35 hot roasted turkey at Thanksgiving, and the French eat hot
roasted goose at Christmas. In Lebanon, however, people might
eat tabouleh (parsley salad) and Baba Ganouj (cold eggplant and
garbanzo dip) to keep cool.

Geography also plays an important role in the foods we choose.
40 Since Japan is surrounded by water, it is not surprising to learn
that the Japanese diet is rich in fish and seaweed. Millet, a type
of grass cultivated for grain, is a basic food in Africa, where it is
plentiful; but it is regarded as undesirable in other places where it
is used as birdseed. Also, in very hot countries it is not unusual
45 to discover that most food is highly spiced. The reason for this is
because before refrigeration, spice was used to cover up the
strong taste food developed in the heat before it spoiled.

Folklore and myth play important roles in the foods we select
for celebrations and feasts. In Greece, for instance, a cake
50 containing a single silver coin is served on New Year's Day.
Whoever finds the coin in his or her serving is said to have good
luck throughout the coming year. In other Mediterranean
countries, people observe similar customs—hiding a dry bean, a
ring, or some other object. Similarly, in the U.S. Southerners
55 traditionally eat black-eyed peas, cornbread, and mustard greens
on New Year's Day to bring good luck in the coming year. At
birthday celebrations in Japan, lobster is the traditional birthday
food, because its shape is thought to resemble someone growing
old and bent over. The birthday person who is being served
60 lobster is being wished a long life.

As people continue to move from country to country, taking
their food and customs with them, people will become familiar
with each other's customs. As a result, our food choices will
grow. Before long, it may be just as common to eat octopus in
65 the United States as it is in Greece or Spain, or to enjoy tacos
and mole from Mexico in Turkey or Korea.

 EXERCISE 1: *Meaning from Context*

*Use the context to figure out the meanings of the words. Write
definitions on a sheet of paper.*

1. motivate *(line 13)*   **3.** accustomed to *(line 33)*   **5.** resemble *(line 58)*
2. reward *(line 26)*   **4.** undesirable *(line 43)*   **6.** bent over *(line 59)*

📖 **EXERCISE 2:** *Food and Culture*

*Organize the information in the reading by filling in the chart. Fill
in the information about the four foods. Then add three more
from the reading. Work from memory, if possible.*

Food	Culture	Reason Used
roasted turkey		
millet		
tabouleh		
lobster		

📖 **EXERCISE 3:** *Comprehension Check*

Answer the questions from memory, if possible.

1. In what parts of the world do people enjoy eating
grasshoppers and termites?
2. If an American says, "I could eat a horse," what does the
person mean?
3. Why do people find certain foods comforting?
4. How does climate and weather affect our food choices?
5. What are some foods people think bring good luck?
6. Why will our food choices continue to grow?

EXERCISE 4: *Find It!*

A. *Review the article. Find related forms of the words in column 1. Write each form and its part of speech in column 2.*

Word	Form(s) and Part(s) of Speech
1. roast	
2. comfort	
3. treat	
4. fry	
5. spice	
6. candy	

B. *Write the correct form of the word on the line.*

1. French **(fry)** _____ potatoes are sliced potatoes cooked in oil.

2. Many North Americans find chicken soup **(comfort)** _____ .

3. **(Roast)** _____ chicken is a traditional Sunday meal in many countries.

4. For her birthday, Maggie had a special **(treat)** _____ —a chocolate cake and ice cream!

5. This soup has no flavor. I wish that I'd ordered something **(spice)** _____ .

DISCUSSION

1. What foods bring back childhood memories for you?

2. Would you eat a caterpillar? Why or why not?

3. What are some foods from other cultures that you like? What do you associate with them?

4. What are some foods you find comforting? Why do you think this is so?

5. What are some foods that are important to your culture because of geography or weather?

WORD FOR WORD!

Describing Objects and Our Reactions to Objects

We can form adjectives from the past participle and present participle forms of many verbs. We use the present participle to describe something. We use the past participle to talk about our reactions to something.

> Melon is very refreshing in summer.
> I ate a piece of melon and felt refreshed.

EXERCISE 5: *That Was Fascinating!*

A. *Write a present participle or a past participle adjective on the line.*

1. I saw a documentary on African food on TV. I was

(fascinate) _____ .

2. Mr. Rowe eats jelly on his eggs. I think that's

(disgust) _____ .

3. Many people think that iced tea is a **(cool)** _____

drink on a hot day.

4. At their dinner party, Bill and Mary served a wonderful dessert—

fried ice cream. All the guests were **(amaze)** _____ .

5. Everyone likes eating, but most people think that washing the

dishes is **(bore)** _____ .

B. *Work with a partner. Imagine that you each just visited another country and had many new and wonderful experiences. Take turns asking and answering questions about each other's experiences. Use present and past participle adjectives.*

A: What did you have to eat?
B: Well, they offered me fried termites. At first, I was surprised. But I tried one. They had a very interesting flavor, so I ate them all!

SPEAK OUT!

Inviting Participation

When we are having a conversation, we try to include everyone who is present in order to be polite. In the conversation, note how the speakers invite others to join in.

JIA: I'm going to make egg rolls for our class potluck dinner. Which do you like better, shrimp or chicken?

IVAN: Both sound delicious! But some people are allergic to shrimp. I know that if Maria eats shrimp, she'll get sick. So why not make chicken?

JIA: Yeah, you're right. What're you bringing?

IVAN: I'm thinking of making feijoada. It's a dish with beans and meat. At home in Brazil we make it with smoked sausage, tongue, and pigs' feet, but here I'll use pork chops.

JIA: Delicious! But a lot of people in our class don't eat pork. Maybe you should make something else.

IVAN: You're right. I'll have to think of something! What about you, Sun-su?

SUN-SU: I'm going to bring a special Korean food—kimchi. It's very spicy! I brought the ingredients from Korea!

JIA: Great! I love spicy food. Look, there's Marta! Hi, Marta. What are you bringing to the class dinner?

MARTA: I don't know what to make. I'd fix a special kind of fruit salad with oranges and nuts if I could find some dried rose petals. But I don't know where to buy them here.

IVAN: I don't know, either. So many things are hard to find here. The teacher said he was going to bring some American food. At least *he* won't have trouble buying the ingredients!

EXERCISE 6: *What About You?*

A. *How did the speakers in the conversation invite each other to participate? Circle the letters.*

a. inviting others to join the group

b. explaining the topic to newcomers

c. asking someone else to speak

d. changing the subject

e. asking for additional information

B. *Work with three other students. Describe the foods your families eat on special occasions and say how they're prepared. Encourage everyone to join the conversation.*

FIGURE IT OUT!

A. *Speculating About the Future*

When we talk about what may happen in the future if a certain condition occurs, we can use the first conditional.

> If Maria eats shrimp, she'll get sick.
> Some people think that if they eat lobster, they'll live for a long time.

EXERCISE 7: *Food Facts*

A. *What effects do different foods have? Finish the sentence.*

1. If you drink coffee, _____ .

2. If you eat too much candy, _____ .

3. If you never drink milk or eat cheese, _____ .

4. You won't get strong if _____ .

5. You might live to a very old age if _____

_____ .

6. If you eat plenty of fruit and vegetables, _____ .

7. You'll get strong if _____ .

B. *Work with a partner. What do you know about the relationship between food and vitamins? Brainstorm a list of foods and the vitamins they contain. Then, using the conditional, make sentences showing the effects of eating or not eating those foods.*

B. *Speculating About the Present and the Past*

When we talk about how things might be different from the way they are right now, we use the second conditional.

Present Situation	Speculation About Present
I don't have any rose petals.	If I had rose petals, I could make a special fruit salad.
Maria is allergic to shrimp.	If Maria weren't allergic to shrimp, Jia could make shrimp egg rolls.

When we want to speculate about how things might have been in the past, we use the third conditional.

Past Situation	Speculation About the Past
I didn't bring any rose petals from my country.	If I'd brought rose petals. I could have made fruit salad.
Maria ate shrimp and got sick.	If she hadn't eaten shrimp, she wouldn't have gotten sick.

EXERCISE 8: *That's a Good Idea!*

Work with a partner. Imagine that you have various problems. Take turns asking for and giving advice. Use the information in Exercise 7.

A: I caught a terrible cold.
B: If you had drunk more orange juice, you wouldn't have caught a cold.

EXERCISE 9: *What a Trip!*

Bill just got back from a vacation in Tolupa, a small island country. Joe is asking him about his trip. Write the correct form of the verb on the line.

JOE: So how was Tolupa? I heard that they eat a lot of different foods there, like insects.

BILL: I heard that, too, but I when I got there, I found out it's not true. But if they **(1. offer)** _____ me insects, I **(2. eat)** _____ them.

JOE: Really! Not me. If I **(3. eat)** _____ an insect, I **(4. get)** _____ sick.

BILL: Don't be so closed-minded. I tried a lot of other Tolupan foods that I thought I'd never eat, like eel.

JOE: Eel!

BILL: That's right. It was delicious. I have a rule when I travel: If the people in that country **(5. eat)** _____ a certain food, I **(6. eat)** _____ it, too. If I **(7. be)** _____ you, I **(8. change)** _____ my attitude about foreign food.

eel:

JOE: You know, you're right. There's a Tolupan restaurant here in town. Let's go for dinner this weekend. If they

(9. have) _____ eel on the menu, I

(10. order) _____ it.

 LISTEN TO THIS!

All of us have favorite foods and foods that we are used to. How do people feel when they try new and different foods? Are some people more open to new experiences than others? Why or why not?

 EXERCISE 10: *Food Talk*

Listen to the radio program and fill in the chart.

Food	Why This Food Surprises Some People
1. Mole	
2.	
3.	
4.	
5.	

 SAY IT CLEARLY!

Intonation

Did you know that some experts think that only 20 percent of what we say is conveyed by words—and that tone and intonation are as important as the actual words we say? For example, the intonation. Listen to the examples. Which one has rising intonation? falling intonation?

> You made cake for dessert! Great!
> The cake fell on the floor! Great!

EXERCISE 11: *Great!*

Listen to the conversations and use intonation to figure out the speakers' feelings. Circle the answer.

1. In conversation 1, Speaker B is   **interested / not interested.**

   The intonation was   **rising / falling.**

2. In conversation 2, Speaker D   **will / will not**   have

   breakfast in the hotel. The intonation was   **rising / falling.**

A. *Work with a partner. Predict whether the intonation will be rising or falling. Write **R** for rising or **F** for falling by the word in **dark type.***

A: Guess **what!** Bill was invited to dinner at the Tolupan Embassy!

B: How **'bout** that!

A: They served eel. He couldn't eat a bite of the food.

B: Oh, **great!**

C: So you went to Eleganza's Restaurant! That's **wonderful!** Is it as good as they say?

D: **Delicious!** Everything was **excellent!** But they wouldn't take our credit cards, so we had to wash the dishes.

C: **Wonderful!**

B. *Listen to the conversations and check your answers.*

C. *Work with a partner. Say the conversations in **A** aloud. Then switch roles and say them aloud again. Pay attention to the intonation.*

 READ ABOUT IT!

Predicting from Topic Sentences

One way to figure out what a reading will be about is by making predictions from the topic sentences. Read the topic sentences of the article on yogurt. What do you think the article will be about? In what ways do you think that yogurt is an amazing food?

90° to 100° F = 32° to 37° C

If there is such a thing as a wonder food, yogurt would surely earn that name. Associated everywhere with long life, yogurt is nutritionally superior to ordinary milk in many ways. In fact, in many parts of the world, this is the only form in which milk is consumed.

The benefits of yogurt are almost limitless. If one to three cups of yogurt are eaten daily, some kinds of infection clear up quickly. Yogurt also aids the digestion of iron. Have you ever tried yogurt as a face mask? Its astringent qualities are a help to oily skin.

Yogurt is easy to make at home. Here's a simple way to make it, if you don't have a yogurt maker. Heat fresh milk to "hand hot," about 90° to 100°. To this very warm milk, add about three tablespoons of yogurt (for one quart of milk). Stir it into the milk and pour it all at once into a wide-mouthed thermos jar. Cover it tightly and let it stand overnight. Next morning, the yogurt is thick and creamy; uncap it and refrigerate it right away.

EXERCISE 13: *Using Topic Sentences*

1. Did the topic sentences give you accurate clues about the content of the reading?

2. Did reading the topic sentences help you read the article more quickly and with better comprehension?

EXERCISE 14: *Recognizing Cause and Effect*

*What are the benefits of yogurt? Write sentences with **if** on the lines.*

1. _____

2. _____

3. _____

DISCUSSION

1. Have you heard of any other foods that people think have amazing effects? Do you believe that they really have these effects?

2. Is food only for eating? What other uses can food have?

SPEAK OUT!

Asking for Clarification

When we exchange detailed information, such as the steps in a recipe, we often have to ask for clarification in order to get the exact information we need. What language is used to ask for clarification? Underline the words and expressions.

A: I'm not clear on what "hand hot" means.
B: It means warm, but not very warm. If you put a finger in the milk, it shouldn't get burned.
A: Could you explain something else? Where should I let it stand?
B: Well, any warm, safe place in your kitchen, really. I put mine in the oven, but I don't turn it on. The inside of the oven is usually a little warmer than the rest of the house, and no one will disturb it.
A: What if someone wants to use the oven?
B: Well, if you're afraid that someone will turn on the oven while the yogurt is in there, write a note and put it on the controls of the oven!

EXERCISE 15: *I Have a Question*

Think of your favorite dish. Work with a partner. Take turns explaining to each other how to make your favorite dishes. As your partner is explaining, ask for clarification as necessary.

WRITE ABOUT IT!

Transition Words and Phrases

In good paragraph writing, it is important to move smoothly from sentence to sentence. We can use transitional words and phrases such as **first, then, in addition, on the other hand,** and **as a result** to make our writing more effective.

 EXERCISE 16: *In the First Place, . . .*

Write the transitional words or phrases in the correct places in the chart.

the effect was	**first**	**than**
at the beginning	**also**	**last**
in the first place	**second**	**and**
as a consequence	**instead**	**in addition**
to start with	**as a result**	**consequently**
in contrast	**on one hand**	**on the other hand**

addition	
cause/effect	
chronological order	
compare/contrast	

 EXERCISE 17: *My Favorite Holiday Food*

A. *Think about your favorite holiday food. Answer the questions on a sheet of paper.*

1. What is its history? Where does it come from? How is it made? What is its value in your culture?
2. What are its special qualities? What makes it different from other foods? Why do you like it? Why might other people not like it?
3. What would you do if you moved to a place where you couldn't get this food?

B. *Use your ideas to write a paragraph about your favorite food on a sheet of paper. Use transitional devices in your paragraph to move from sentence to sentence.*

C. *Show your paragraph to a partner to edit for content, clarity, and organization. Then write your final draft.*

UNIT 7 Roll Over, Beethoven!

THINK ABOUT IT!

A. Look at the types of music in the box. What kind of music do you prefer for each of the activities in the list?

jazz	reggae
classical	disco
heavy metal	hip hop
folk	gospel
rock and roll	rap
country and western	soul

relaxing   studying   driving   working
dancing   cleaning   exercising   falling to sleep

B. Has your taste in music changed over the years? Why or why not?

TALK IT OVER!

A. Work with a small group. Find out who has seen a music festival, show, or concert. Who performed? What happened? What was the best part of the event? What was the atmosphere like? the lighting? Were there costumes? Was there make-up? What was the mood of the audience?

B. Is the message of music in the words or in the performance? Does the image of the singer or the group influence your choice of music?

READ ABOUT IT!

Using Structure to Anticipate Meaning

The introduction of an article usually prepares the reader for the exposition of the article, and the conclusion summarizes its main points. Focusing in on these items as well as the first sentence of each body paragraph gives the reader a quick overall view of the text. Follow this procedure as you look at the article on pages 75 and 76. Then circle the letter of the correct answer.

1. The article is about
   a. different types of popular music people listen to.
   b. musicians who influenced rock and roll.
   c. clubs and discos where pop groups played.

2. The information is organized
   a. chronologically.
   b. by location.
   c. by rank order.

Using Capitalization, Punctuation, and Numbers to Anticipate Meaning

Effective readers also use capitalization, punctuation, names, and numbers to pick up quick clues about the content of a text.

1. *Classify these items that commonly appear in texts in the correct column.*

postal codes	years
coined words	months
book titles	times
addresses	people
money	places
dialogues	countries
days	quotations
nationalities	song titles
percentages	dates

2. *Look through the article and underline the names of musicians you know. Tell a partner what you know about them.*

Capital Letters

Quotation Marks

Numbers

The Beatles   Elvis Presley

Rock and Roll Is Here to Stay!
by D. Michael Cheers

The hazy origin of rock and roll is the subject of much debate and controversy. Some have argued that rock and roll was born in the souls of black people who strummed homemade guitars and sang down-home jazz and blues tunes in clubs all over southern America. Others
5 say this cultural revolution evolved from a combination of black blues, white country, and hillbilly boogie. It was then re-packaged and presented by whites to audiences in the rest of the country.

Alan Freed, a Philadelphia disc jockey, is credited with coining the phrase "rock and roll" in 1951. By the mid-1950s, teenagers could not
10 get enough of the pulsating rhythm. The sound was here to stay.

An array of rockers rode the early wave of rock and roll fame: Bill Haley and the Comets, Fats Domino, the Platters, Chuck Berry, Bo Didley, Buddy Holly, Jerry Lee Lewis, and Ray Charles. But it is Little Richard, who, without much dissent, lays claim to the title "The King of
15 Rock and Roll."

Little Richard first sang gospel music and learned to play the piano in a neighborhood church. But somewhere in his soul, the immortal sounds "Awopbopaloobop-alopbamboom! Tutti Frutti! Aw rootie" waited to be born. After hits like "Tutti Frutti," "Long Tall Sally," and "Good

20 Golly, Miss Molly,'' Little Richard left rock and roll and turned to gospel singing. He returned in the 1960s and has remained on the rock music scene ever since.

Another man who would later be revered as a cult figure and then an icon, as a teen, had an uninspiring hillbilly voice. But what
25 Elvis Aron Presley lacked in his singing style, he made up in physical appeal. His twists and shouts on stage sent females in the audience into a frenzy. In 1954 a *Billboard* Poll named the young Presley ''most promising hillbilly artist.'' It wasn't long before the nation began to swoon over the boy from Tupelo,
30 Mississippi. Presley recorded a string of hits that began with ''Heartbreak Hotel,'' the first in an incredible series of fourteen consecutive million-record sellers that included ''Hound Dog'' and ''Blue Suede Shoes.'' In addition, television allowed Presley to reach millions of viewers. Unfortunately, at that time, black rock
35 and roll artists of equal and superior talents such as Willie Mae Thorton, Sam Cooke, and James Brown were not offered any lucrative recording contracts, nor invited to appear on television. Their ''original'' rock and roll was still heard mostly on low frequency black radio stations and in segregated towns in the
40 south.

Across the Atlantic Ocean in the port city of Liverpool, England, another cultural phenomenon was brewing. The Beatles—John Lennon, Paul McCartney, George Harrison, and Ringo Starr—were playing gigs around England for sixty pounds a night. Their appeal
45 to British youngsters was astonishing. The American television host Ed Sullivan was at a London airport and saw a near riot of Beatles fans that convinced him to put the group on his weekly show. Sullivan booked the Beatles for three consecutive weeks. In all, some 73 million Americans saw the show on television and
50 thrilled to ''Twist and Shout'' and ''I Want to Hold Your Hand.'' Shortly after, the Beatles had five singles simultaneously on *Billboard's* ''Hot 100'' charts.

This group, influenced by the music of the Four Seasons, the Isley Brothers, Buddy Holly, Otis Redding, and Little Richard, was
55 followed by others also influenced by black musicians—the Rolling Stones, the Animals, Big Brother and the Holding Company with Janis Joplin, Cream, the Allman Brothers, and the Grateful Dead, to name but a few. All these musicians and many others have left an indelible impact on the cultural frenzy called rock and roll.

Janis Joplin

Ray Charles

DISCUSSION

1. Imagine a time without TV. How did people learn about new singers?

2. Are singers from different cultures treated differently as performers today?

3. What are the titles of current hits? What are they about?

EXERCISE 1: *Meaning from Context*

Match the words in column 1 with the meanings in column 2. Write the
letter on the line. Compare your answers with a partner's.

_____	**1.** hazy *(line 1)*	**a.**	attraction
_____	**2.** strummed *(line 3)*	**b.**	effect
_____	**3.** evolved *(line 5)*	**c.**	unclear, unidentified
_____	**4.** coining *(line 8)*	**d.**	inventing
_____	**5.** array *(line 11)*	**e.**	excited, wild actions
_____	**6.** appeal *(line 26)*	**f.**	developed
_____	**7.** frenzy *(lines 27, 59)*	**g.**	amazing
_____	**8.** segregated *(line 39)*	**h.**	variety, range
_____	**9.** astonishing *(line 45)*	**i.**	played
_____	**10.** impact *(line 59)*	**j.**	separated into black and white

EXERCISE 2: *Understanding Chronology*

The article tells us some of the history of rock and roll. Using facts from
the article and your own knowledge, match the dates with the events.
Write the correct letter on the line. Then compare your ideas with those
of a partner.

1. _____ In 1951

2. _____ In 1954

3. _____ In the mid 50s

4. _____ In the 1960s

5. _____ In April, 1964

6. _____ In 1977

7. _____ In 1980

a. John Lennon was shot in New York.

b. Alan Freed coined "rock and roll."

c. Little Richard returned to the music scene.

d. Elvis Presley died and became a cult figure.

e. American teenagers were crazy about rock and roll music.

f. The Beatles held the five top places in the charts.

g. Elvis Presley was called "the most promising hillbilly artist."

(left) Strawberry Fields   (right) Elvis Presley's grave

EXERCISE 3: *Opinions*

A. The first paragraph of the article says that there are two opinions on
the origin of rock and roll. What are they? Complete the sentences.

Some have argued _____

_____ .

Others say _____

_____ .

B. What is the writer's opinion? How do you know? Compare your
ideas with those of a partner.

WORD FOR WORD!

 EXERCISE 4: *Read It and Weep!*

What do the two- and three-word verbs in the letter mean? Use the context to match the word or expression with its meaning.

_____ **a.** discovered

_____ **b.** depending on

_____ **c.** couldn't see at all

_____ **d.** took in a car

_____ **e.** hurry from

_____ **f.** reach

_____ **g.** got separated

_____ **h.** finished

_____ **i.** quickly went to

_____ **j.** obtain

_____ **k.** get across

_____ **l.** stopped thinking of

_____ **m.** leaving

_____ **n.** walked about

> Dear Michelle,
>
> You know I told you in my last letter that my girlfriend had managed to **(1)** *pick up* two tickets for the Rod Stalwart concert. Well, the concert was last night, and you just won't believe what happened! After the concert **(2)** *was over*, everyone started to **(3)** *rush out* of the stadium, and we **(4)** *split up.* I tried to **(5)** *work through* the crowd to **(6)** *get to* her, but I **(7)** *lost sight* of her completely. I **(8)** *wandered around* looking for her for hours, it seemed, but suddenly I **(9)** *forgot about* her entirely, because I actually saw Rod **(10)** *coming out* of the stadium! I **(11)** *ran up* to him to ask for his autograph, and he could see I was upset about something. When he **(12)** *found out* I had lost the ride home I **(13)** *was counting on,* he actually **(14)** *drove me back!* Can you stand it! The local paper wrote about it and everything! I'm including a copy of the article so you can read all about it.
>
> Love,
> Donna

 # SPEAK OUT!

Expressing Preferences and Opinions

Just as we all know what we like to eat, we are usually very clear about our "taste" in music. We express our preferences and opinions, and often we compare and contrast different types of music. In the conversation, underline the words and expressions that signal preferences and opinions.

AL: Hi, Joe. What are you listening to?

JOE: One of my old favorites, Pink Floyd. This album is "The Dark Side of the Moon."

AL: So you're wild about it?

JOE: Yeah, I love it. It's one of those albums that I can put on anytime and feel. . . .

AL: Feel what?

JOE: Oh, melancholy, a bit sad, you know, but excited, too. It makes me want to dance, and it brings back memories.

AL: What memories?

JOE: Oh, things that were happening in my life at that time, memories of an old girlfriend. Don't you feel the same?

AL: Yeah. I find it's not so much the song itself, but a reflection of what was going on in my life then—sort of "history" music. I don't really enjoy music so much until later, when it makes me remember things. For easy listening, though, I really like country and western.

JOE: I don't mind listening to it for fun, but it doesn't do anything for me emotionally. It doesn't move me.

AL: What do you think about rap then?

JOE: I don't really care for it. It's important culturally, as a social statement of the times, but it's more like poetry than music. My taste is more for groups like Jethro Tull and Genesis, who were classically trained. They went through music school. I go for that sort of sound rather than simple beats and lyrics from groups that just somehow picked up music and played together.

Queen Latifah, rap artist

EXERCISE 5: *I Know What I Like*

Work with a partner. Use words and expressions from the conversation and the list to talk about your own musical tastes. Explain why you like the kinds of music you do, and compare and contrast them with the kinds you don't particularly like. Are your tastes similar? different?

+	**o**	**−**
love/adore	don't mind	hate/detest
really like	quite like	don't care for it at all
very fond of	can take it	can't stand it
enjoy it a lot	or leave it	can't bear it
crazy about	it's all right	really loathe

EXERCISE 6: *I'd Choose. . . .*

Interview three students in your class. Ask them which two pieces of music they would take if they had to live alone on an island and why. Fill in the chart with their answers.

Choices	Reasons
1.	
2.	
3.	

FIGURE IT OUT!

A. Relative Pronouns and Relative Clauses

As you know, a relative pronoun usually introduces a relative clause which gives us more information about the noun in the main clause. Relative pronouns can be used as subjects or objects.

Relative pronouns as subject:
I don't care for music **that** puts me to sleep.
I like music **which** sounds new and exciting.
I enjoy a singer **who** puts a lot of energy into a song.

Relative pronouns as object:
The music video **that** we saw on TV was great!
The concert **which** we attended was sold out.
The stereo (no pronoun) I bought was on sale.
The gospel singer **who(m)** we listened to was very moving.
The rock star **who** we asked for an autograph ignored us.
The heavy metal group (no pronoun) we saw was fabulous.

EXERCISE 7: *It's All Relative*

Complete the sentence with your own opinion. Circle all the relative pronouns that can be used in your sentences.

1. I like music that/which/who/whom/(no pronoun) _____

_____ .

2. The radio station that/which/who/whom/(no pronoun) I like best is _____

_____ .

3. I listen to groups that/which/who/whom/(no pronoun) _____

_____ .

4. The songs that/which/who/whom/(no pronoun) bring back good memories for me are _____

_____ .

B. Restrictive and Non-Restrictive Clauses

1. Restrictive clauses give us essential information about the noun in the main clause. We don't use commas to set off the clause because the information it gives defines the noun.

The singer **who was named "most promising" in 1954** was Elvis Presley.

2. Non-restrictive clauses give us additional information about the noun in the main clause. We use commas to set off the clause because it does not contain information that defines the noun. When speaking, we pause at the commas.

Elvis Presley, **who grew up in a small town,** became a world-famous rock star.

EXERCISE 8: *Essential or Additional Information?*

Read each sentence and decide if the clause gives essential or additional information. Put in commas if necessary.

1. Black people who strummed guitars in southern clubs created rock and roll.
2. Little Richard who was first a gospel singer was later popular with both black and white listeners.
3. At that time local radio stations played music for audiences who were segregated.
4. The *Billboard* Poll of 1954 which predicted Elvis Presley's success was right.

C. The restrictive/non-restrictive distinction sometimes influences meaning. Study the sentences in the box. What is the difference in meaning? Write the correct sentence number on the line.

> 1. The students who like pop music went to the concert.
> 2. The students, who like pop music, went to the concert.

Sentence _____ means that only some of the students—those who like pop music—went to the concert.
Sentence _____ means that all the students like pop music and they all went to the concert.

 EXERCISE 9: *All or Some?*

Read the sentences and put in commas if necessary. Then work with a partner and take turns reading the sentences aloud. Be sure to communicate the meaning of "all" or "some" as the correct punctuation dictates.

1. The fans loved the Beatles' songs which were hits.
2. The fans who traveled from all over the country went crazy at the concert.
3. The clubs which admitted fifteen-year-olds made a lot of money.
4. The club owners who played currently popular music made the most money.
5. The fans who waited for hours to buy tickets began to clap and scream when the band appeared on stage.
6. Concert security guards who showed great patience kept the fans back from the stage.

LISTEN TO THIS!

A. Rock and roll has developed in several different directions since its beginnings. There are now many different sub-classifications of rock and roll, such as hard rock, punk rock, heavy metal, new age progressive rock, and rockabilly. What do you know about them?

B. How does a rock group form, practice, get needed exposure in the musical world, and finally become famous? Share your ideas.

Aerosmith

EXERCISE 10: *Aerosmith*

A. *Listen to the radio report on the rock group Aerosmith and order the events in the list chronologically. Number them from* **1** *(first) to* **7** *(last).*

_____ The band records the critically aclaimed album "Pump."
_____ Drummer Joey Kramer invents the band name "Aerosmith."
_____ The band moves to Boston, which becomes their home base.
_____ Columbia Records releases the album "Greatest Hits."
_____ The band performs at Nipmuc Regional High School.
_____ The band has problems that lead to a loss of popularity.
_____ Lead singer Steve Tyler and guitarist Joe Perry reunite.

B. *Work with a partner. Summarize the most important information from the radio report.*

SAY IT CLEARLY!

There are many varieties of English, as different as the countries, regions, and people that speak them. Songs show the range of possible variations, and often contain examples of reductions, syllable additions, and nonstandard English. Look at the song titles in the box.

reduction:	"We Got**ta** Get Out of This Place"
syllable addition:	"Train Kept **a**-Rollin"
nonstandard English:	"You Never **Done** It Like That"

EXERCISE 11: *Name That Tune!*

Classify the song titles as examples of reduction, syllable addition, or nonstandard English. Write **R** *for reduction,* **SA** *for syllable addition, or* **NS** *for nonstandard on the line.*

_____ "I'm Gonna Play the Honky-Tonks"
_____ "Ain't No Mountain High Enough"
_____ "Bout Changes 'n' Things"
_____ "Baby, I'm-a Want You"
_____ "You Was Up"
_____ "Rockin' Pneumonia and the Boogie Woogie Flu"
_____ "Sh-Boom"
_____ "Sho Feels Good to Me"

EXERCISE 12: *Gotta Get Going*

Work with a partner. Take turns reading the conversation aloud. Try to use the reduced form of the words in dark type. When you finish, listen to check your pronunciation of the reductions.

A: It's really late. I've **got to** get **going.**
B: Where **are you going** in such a hurry?
A: I've got a ticket to a rock concert, and I **want to** get there as soon as I can. **You know** how the lines can be at a concert!
B: I hear **you.** Well, better get **moving,** then. You **should have** left before now.
A: Yeah. Now I'll **have to** wait in line for sure.

READ ABOUT IT!

Use the photos and the title of the article to predict what the article will be about. Then brainstorm a list of vocabulary words that will probably appear in the text.

Jimi Hendrix

Rock Tragedies
by D. Michael Cheers

Is there a tragic destiny awaiting those musicians who dedicate their lives to rock and roll? Throughout the years many rock greats have suffered tragic and even cruel deaths.

Both Buddy Holly and Ritchie Valens were riding the crest of success when on a wintry February night in 1959 following a concert in Clear Lake, Iowa, the two rising stars boarded a chartered plane headed for Fargo, North Dakota. The plane crashed in a cornfield and everyone on board died on impact.

At the time of Holly's death, he was just beginning a solo career. His latest record "It Doesn't Matter Anymore" had just hit the record stores. Valens, a Mexican-American, was flying high off his recently released single "La Bamba."

In 1970, while the music world was still recovering from the shock of the loss of guitar genius Jimi Hendrix, declared dead on arrival at a London hospital, news came of another rock star's demise just three weeks later. Janis Joplin, just reaching her powerful musical maturity, was found dead in a Los Angeles motel room.

Otis Redding

Another great cut down before his time was Elvis Presley, who expired in 1977 in Memphis, Tennessee, a victim of congestive heart failure and advanced arteriosclerosis. Presley's death inspired his fans to hold permanent vigils at his Graceland gravesite in Memphis.

The list of rock tragedies was lengthened the night of December 8, 1980, when John Lennon of the Beatles was fatally shot seven times outside the Dakota apartment building in New York, by an over-zealous Beatles fan.

Blues guitarist great Stevie Ray Vaughan met his untimely end in August of 1990. After performing with his brother Jimmie, Eric Clapton, and Buddy Guy at a concert in Alpine Valley, Wisconsin, Vaughan boarded a helicopter to Chicago. He never made it; the helicopter crashed and Stevie did not survive.

Music historians have said that the night of Holly's crash was "the day the music died." The music in fact did not die, but these sudden and tragic losses of some of rock and roll's true greats did indeed cause the music to skip a beat. However, the music has continued. The night following the deaths of Holly and Valens, Frankie Avalon and Jimmy Clanton replaced them on tour. Elvis and his music live today through his films and re-releases of his hit records. John Lennon's wife, Yoko Ono, and his sons Sean and Julian, carry on his tradition. Jimmie Vaughan continues to play his guitar in memory of his brother, and the album on which they collaborated has become a hit. Indeed, the beat goes on!

DISCUSSION

1. Why do so many singers and performers seem to adopt wild lifestyles and live so dangerously?

2. Do singers and other artists need to suffer to create their art?

3. Do you know of any other rock tragedies? Explain.

Paraphrasing

As you know, paraphrasing is retelling information we have read or heard in our own words. We keep the main ideas but state them differently. Which is the better paraphrase for the last paragraph of the article? Circle the number.

1. The music didn't die with the people but continued with other singers. Historians remember times when the music skipped a beat, and they remind us that Lennon's sons carry on his tradition, and Jimmie Vaughan had a great hit.

2. Although these famous rock stars died tragically and unexpectedly, we remember their music through their friends or families who continue their work, or through their movies and records that we can still enjoy.

 SPEAK OUT!

Using Euphemisms

Depending on the subject we are dealing with, we sometimes avoid using the most direct way of saying something because the words seem too strong or possibly insensitive. Many people, for example, prefer not to use the words **die** and **death.**

 EXERCISE 13: *In Other Words*

A. *Of the examples related to death listed here, which are used in the article on rock tragedies? Do you know any other euphemisms related to the idea of death?*

demise	untimely end	cut down before (his) time	deceased	left this world
loss	gone to a better place	passed away	was taken	expired

B. *Another sensitive area is that of being out of work. Work with a partner. How many ways can you think of to communicate the ideas of* **losing a job** *and* **getting fired** *in a less direct way?*

 WRITE ABOUT IT!

Multi-Paragraph Writing

Just as a well-organized single paragraph contains a topic sentence, supporting sentences, and a concluding sentence, an essay, or group of paragraphs about one topic, contains similar organizing devices. The **introductory paragraph** tells us what the writer is going to write about. It is followed by one or more paragraphs called the **body** of the essay. These paragraphs develop and support ideas related to the main topic of the essay. The **concluding paragraph** sums up the main ideas developed and brings the essay to an end. This organizational pattern is equally effective in essays expressing an opinion, showing a comparison and contrast, or explaining a problem and developing a solution. Look at the model of an essay on page 86 and label the introductory paragraph, the body, and the concluding paragraph.

(title) ~~~~~~

I personally believe that music videos have ruined the music industry. Before the advent of music videos, song lyrics, together with the melody, allowed the listener the use of his or her own imagination. ~~~~~~
~~~~~~
~~~~~~

Nowadays, music lovers are forced to picture the images of someone else's mind. ~~~~~~~~~~~~~~~~~~~~~~~~~~~~~~~~~~~~~~~
~~~~~~
~~~~~~

In addition, the visual presentation of the song may, in fact, have nothing to do with the lyrics. ~~~~~~~~~~~~~~~~~~~~~~~~~~~~~
~~~~~~
~~~~~~

It is therefore clear to me that the visual manipulation of our minds by video producers is harmful to the music industry and music lovers everywhere. ~~~~~~~~~~~~~~~~~~~~~~~~~~~~~~~~~~~~~
~~~~~~
~~~~~~

EXERCISE 14: *Let's Rock and Roll!*

A. *Develop a model of an essay similar to the example, using the first sentence as the essay topic. Write one more sentence for your introductory paragraph, a topic sentence for each of your body paragraphs, and a sentence for your concluding paragraph. Write on a separate sheet of paper.*

Winning two tickets to a dream rock and roll concert by a favorite group is not the best thing that can happen to a fan. ~~~~~~~
~~~~~~
~~~~~~

B. Work with a partner. Exchange papers and check the organization and clarity of your written ideas. Did you develop sentences for each paragraph that were related to the overall main idea given in the first sentence? Did you write a sentence clearly showing the essay is coming to an end? Did you choose ideas to develop in each paragraph that you can easily support with additional sentences?

C. After your partner has commented on your work, finish your essay by adding the supporting sentences necessary to complete each idea you have that is related to the main idea of the essay.

UNIT 8 *You're Just My Type!*

 ## THINK ABOUT IT!

A. What kind of person are you? If you were asked to list three adjectives that describe your personality, what would they be?

B. What kind of person do you want other people to think you are? Is your answer the same for all of the people you meet? List three adjectives that describe the kind of person you'd like the people in the chart to think you are. Then compare your answer with a partner's.

A Job Interviewer	A New Friend	A Neighbor

 ## TALK IT OVER!

A. Do you think people can be divided into groups by personality type? Should people be divided up in this way? Discuss your answer with the class.

B. Here are three common ways to divide personality types. Work in small groups. For each pair of words, find out how many people in your group put themselves in each personality type. How many aren't comfortable with either personality type in each pair? Why?

Thinkers/Feelers   Thinkers/Doers   Introverts/Extroverts

C. Work with the other groups in your class. Find out how many students put themselves into each of the categories in each pair. Are the results surprising? Why or why not?

 ## READ ABOUT IT!

Keeping Track of Details

In reading a longer story or article, we may want to use a strategy to help us keep track of important details. These strategies include underlining, highlighting, or marking the text, keeping a mental list, and taking notes. Do you use any of these strategies to keep track of details? Which ones? Do you have a preferred strategy? Do you use different strategies for different kinds of readings? Which strategy would you use for school assignments? newspaper articles? short stories?

As you read the article "Personality's Part and Parcel" on the next page, use one of the strategies to keep track of the pairs of personality types the author mentions. How many pairs can you find?

Recognizing and Understanding Humor

An author can inject humor into writing in a number of different ways. These include relating a funny story, making a joke, using a pun or play on words, and using language in a humorous way, such as using exaggerated or ironic vocabulary. As you read the article, note places where the author is trying to add humor. Write **H** in the margin each time you find something you consider humorous.

Personality's Part and Parcel
by Paul Chance

Some say there are two kinds of people. What kind of people would say that?

"There are," he said, "two kinds of people: idea people and feeling people. I think you're an idea person."

5 My speech professor was trying to cheer me up after one of the more humiliating experiences in a humiliating freshman year. He had this idea that people would become better public speakers if they first practiced doing really silly things in front of a group. He had me stand before the class, one foot in front of the
10 other, and rock back and forth while swinging my arms, ape fashion, and chanting: Aaahhooooo, aaahhoooo." I did it, but I did it with the embarrassed stiffness you might expect from Richard Nixon if you made him moon walk. Like I said, it was humiliating.

The prof's philosophical musings were intended to reassure
15 me. "You'll never make it as an actor," he was saying, "but you might make it in some more bookish occupation." I took the personality assessment in stride and immediately began wondering (as befitted my bookish personality) whether the entire human population could be categorized by this, or any other, two-
20 legged taxonomy. Was it really true that there were only two kinds of people in the world?

I had problems with the feeling and idea pigeonholes right from the start. I couldn't help wondering why, if I was an idea person, I was in danger of flunking out of college. Was it because my
25 classes placed little emphasis on ideas? I did do better in subsequent years, when the ideas became more plentiful and interesting than they had been in my freshman speech class. But somehow the idea-feeling theory of personality seemed to lack predictability.

30 Another problem I ran into was that there were lots of competing theories about the two kinds of people in the world. One familiar idea is that everybody is either an optimist or a pessimist. Optimists are sure that they'll never die, and that if they do die they'll wake up to the glory of heaven. Pessimists are
35 sure that they won't live much longer, and that if they wake up in heaven, they won't like it.

Another theory says that people are either realists or idealists. A realist is a person who knows which side of the bread is buttered; an idealist has more important things to worry about.
40 The consensus is that realists eat better than idealists.

Other folks divide the human race into animal people and plant people, depending on the company they keep. Animal people talk

---

to their furry or feathered companions in melodious tones about everything from the price of cheese to American foreign policy,
45 as if the animals understood every word that was said. Plant people find such displays sentimental and silly, and they expound upon their views in great detail to their annual and perennial friends.

In recent years we've heard a lot about Type A and Type B
50 personalities. Type B people eat lunch at home or in a restaurant and take their time about doing it. Type A people ram down a hot dog while running up an escalator. Type A people work harder at making money than Type B people, but they don't know how to enjoy it. Type B people know how to enjoy money, but aren't
55 sure it's worth the bother to get it.

Of course, the idea that everyone can be tagged with one of two labels doesn't appeal to everybody. There are lots of psychologists, for example, who would argue that there aren't 2 kinds of people, or 6, or 8 or 37. There are as many kinds of
60 people as there are people. And each person may be different people at different times. Being a human being is a complicated business, these psychologists argue, and you cannot arbitrarily squeeze everybody into one of two categories.

Despite these doubts, I think there is some merit to the idea that there are two kinds of people. In fact, I've come up with my
65 own theory. I propose that there are two kinds of people in the world: those who believe there are two kinds of people and those who don't.

I place myself in the second category. How about you?

DISCUSSION

1. Is it a good idea to put people in groups by personality type? Why or why not?

2. What do you think the author's opinion of psychologists is? Why?

3. What is the author's final assertion about personality types? Do you agree with it? Why or why not?

EXERCISE 1: *Meaning from Context*

These definitions correspond to words in the article. Find the words they define and write them on the lines.

1. _____: embarrassing, causing shame
2. _____: divided into groups by kind or type
3. _____: following; later
4. _____: opinion held by a lot of people
5. _____: difficult because there are a lot of parts or sides or ideas
6. _____: without a thought out reason or a plan
7. _____: put, fit

EXERCISE 2: *An Eye for Detail*

A. *How many different pairs of personality types did you find? How did you keep track of them? Did keeping track of the pairs help you read better? How?*

B. *Work in a group. What strategies did they use to keep track of details? Which strategy was the most popular?*

EXERCISE 3: *That's a Laugh!*

A. *Look at the sixth and seventh paragraphs of the article (lines 30–40). Which parts of the paragraphs are intended to be humorous? How do you know? Share your ideas with the class.*

B. *What makes the parts you chose in* **A** *humorous? Do they tell a funny story? Do they use language in a funny way? What other parts of the article did you find humorous? Share your ideas with a partner.*

C. *What is the tone of the article? What does the tone indicate about the attitude toward the subject? Is it serious, skeptical, or somewhere in between?*

 WORD FOR WORD

Idioms That Describe Personality

As you know, English has many idiomatic expressions. In Unit 1, you studied idioms having to do with animals. In this unit you will learn some idioms used to describe personality.

EXERCISE 4: *As Happy As a Clam!*

Use the context to figure out the meaning of the expression in **dark type.** *Write the letter of the definition on the line.*

a. silent; never makes noise
b. boring
c. a person who dampens other people's enthusiasm
d. intelligent
e. cooperative
f. a person who gets into accidents easily
g. very pleased and excited

_____ **1.** Alan always does the same thing on weekends. All he wants to do is stay home and watch TV. He's **a real stick-in-the-mud.**

_____ **2.** Mimi just got a new job, and a big increase in pay. She's all smiles today. I'll bet she's **as happy as a clam.**

_____ **3.** Don't take Tony shopping for dishes with you. He'll probably drop something expensive and break it. He's **as clumsy as an ox.**

_____ **4.** John and I thought it would be fun to order a pizza and stay up late to laugh and talk, but Sandra didn't want to, so we all went home. Sometimes she's **a real wet blanket.**

_____ **5.** Jack gets along well with everyone, and he's great to work with. He never tries to tell anyone what to do, either. He's really **a team player.**

_____ **6.** Luisa is **as quiet as a mouse!** I didn't even know she'd come in!

SPEAK OUT!

Tactfully Expressing or Softening a Negative Opinion

When we want to express a negative opinion, we often soften it by choosing descriptive words carefully, or by using polite language. When someone else voices a negative opinion, we also may want to restate it in a more tactful way to soften the criticism or to avoid agreeing with such a negative opinion.

Which statements are strongly negative? Which statements are more tactful?

1. She's very unfriendly and abrupt.
2. She seems to be very direct.
3. He seems to be angry all the time.
4. He seems to be worried about a lot of problems.

Expressing Tentative Statements

You may recall from a previous unit that when we make a statement, express an opinion, or give an answer, we may not be completely sure that we are right. We may also have doubts about someone else's information. Our choice of words is determined by how politely we want to express our tentative statement. What words do the speakers in the conversation use to make tentative statements?

SUE: I just met our new neighbor. He was just about to get in his car.

BILL: Oh, really? I talked to him for a while yesterday. What did you think?

SUE: Well, he seemed awfully quiet. I wasn't sure he really wanted to talk.

BILL: Really? Gosh, that's not the impression I got. He came right up to me and introduced himself. He seemed really interested in the neighborhood.

SUE: Maybe, but I couldn't get him to talk about himself at all. I'm not sure, but he didn't seem very outgoing.

BILL: Hmmm. He told me quite a bit about his family and his background. Actually, we talked for almost an hour, I think.

SUE: Really! Are we talking about the same person? I wonder why he seemed so cold to me?

BILL: Maybe he's shy.

SUE: Oh, I doubt it. Not if he talked to you for so long yesterday. He just seemed like he was in a hurry and too busy to talk. And I don't think I asked him more than a couple of questions.

BILL: Wait a minute. Did you say you just talked to him?

SUE: Yes. Why?

BILL: I'm not sure I'm remembering right, but I think he said he had to pick up his wife and kids at the airport this afternoon. They're flying in from where they used to live.

SUE: Oh, that would explain it! Now that you mention it, he did look like he was rushing to do something. You know those things I said? Well, I take them all back. I think I'll go home and make them a housewarming cake.

BILL: See you later, Sue.

EXERCISE 5: *What Did You Think?*

A. *What expressions did Bill and Sue use to tactfully express or soften a negative opinion? What expressions did they use to express tentativeness? Underline them.*

B. *Restate these negative opinions more tactfully. Write sentences on a sheet of paper.*

1. His desk is always a mess.
2. He never arrives on time.
3. She drives much too fast.
4. She always interrupts people to express her ideas.

 EXERCISE 6: *What Was He Like?*

A. *Look at Van Gogh's self-portrait. What might his personality have been like? Include three positive and three negative sides to his personality.*

B. *Discuss your ideas about Van Gogh's personality with a partner. Be sure to be tactful when you are negative and to express doubts when you are not sure.*

C. *Brainstorm the names of four famous people in the news. Do you think their public personalities are different from their private ones? What positive and negative personality aspects do they have? Use the language for expressing a negative opinion and the language for expressing tentativeness when appropriate.*

(G) FIGURE IT OUT!

A. *Separable and Non-Separable Two- and Three-Word Verbs*

There are a number of expressions in English made up of a verb and one or more words, usually prepositions. These are called two- and three-word verbs. You may recall from Unit 4 that the meaning of the verb-preposition combination is different from the normal meanings of the verb and prepositions(s). How many two- and three-word verbs can you find in the article on pages 88 and 89 and the conversation on page 91?

> I **found out** the truth.
> I **got up** early.

Two-word verbs in English may be separable or non-separable.

Separable Two-Word Verbs	
Please **fill out** this form. Please **fill** this form **out**.	Please **fill** it **out.**
Throw away that old shoe! **Throw** that old shoe **away!**	**Throw** it **away!**

Some common separable two-word verbs:

bring back a book	return
call up a person	call on the telephone
cheer up a person	make happy
cross out an answer	write an **X** through
figure out a problem	find an answer
fill in a form	write information in
fill up a bottle	fill completely
find out some information	discover
give back something	return
leave out some information	not include
look up a word	find in a reference book
pick up a book	lift/get from somewhere
pick out a new shirt	choose, select
put down a book	put on a table or the floor
put on a shirt	start wearing
put out the trash	take out of the house
turn off a light	stop it
take off a shirt	stop wearing
think over a request	think about
throw away an old shoe	put in the trash
turn on a light	start it
write down some information	make a note of it

Non-Separable Two- and Three-Word Verbs	
I **ran into** George downtown.	I **ran into** him downtown.
Bill **looks up to** Mary.	Bill **looks up to** her.
Ellen is **looking for** her dog.	Ellen is **looking for** it.

Some common non-separable two- and three-word verbs:

call on someone	visit
come up with an idea	think of
count on someone	depend on
flunk out of school	fail at
get along with someone	enjoy being with
get back from somewhere	return from
get over an illness	recover from
get through with something	finish
look down on someone	not respect
look for someone/something	try to find
put up with someone	tolerate
run into someone	meet unexpectedly
run out of something	have no more of it
stay away from something	avoid

📖📑🗣️ **EXERCISE 7:** *That's Just the Way She Is!*

A. *Complete each of the two- or three-word verbs appropriately with a preposition and a noun or a pronoun. Use pronouns whenever you can.*

Peggy is a pretty easy going person. She likes people; her ability to get **(1)** _____ is above average. She's a good conversationalist. She knows lots of interesting stories and good jokes—She never runs **(2)** _____ . When she gets angry with someone, which isn't often, she always gets **(3)** _____ right away.

She's really friendly, and she's met a lot of people since she moved here. She runs **(4)** _____ all the time when she goes out. Some of the people she knows aren't as interesting or as rich as she is, but she doesn't look **(5)** _____ . When she's at home, she spends a lot of time calling **(6)** _____ on the phone and talking for hours. Everyone loves to hear **(7)** _____ . She's so much fun to talk to!

B. *Write a paragraph describing yourself. Do not write your name. Then pass in your paper and take another student's paper. Work in a small group. Read the paper you get to the group and try to decide who wrote it. Help the other students figure out who wrote their papers.*

B. *Emphatic Do*

Using emphatic **do** is a way to add emphasis to an idea. We often use emphatic **do** to show that we are making an exception to something that is usually true, or to show a contrast between two ideas or situations.

> I have never believed in classifying people by personality type. But I **did** take one of those personality tests the other day, just for fun. And some of what it said **does** make sense. I do better at word games and puzzles than at sports, I **do** enjoy spending time alone, and I am good at math.

📖🗣️ **EXERCISE 8:** *It Does Make Sense!*

A. *What can you conclude about the use of emphatic **do** from the example paragraph? Circle the answer.*

1. For emphasis, a form of the verb **do** can be **added to / substituted for** the main verb in a sentence.

2. With the verb **be,** emphatic **do   is / isn't** used.

B. *Find two examples of emphatic **do** in the article "Personality's Part and Parcel." What contrast or exception is the author making in each one? Discuss your answers with a partner.*

LISTEN TO THIS!

Were you the oldest child in your family, the youngest, in the middle, or an only child? Did this make a difference in your personality? in your brothers' and sisters' personalities? Do you notice similar differences in other children you know?

 EXERCISE 9: *That's Me!*

A. *Listen to the conversation and circle the letter of the correct answer.*

1. The people are talking about
 a. their birthdays.
 b. how many children there are in their families.
 c. the order in which they were born in their families.

2. According to the book they are looking at, people's personalities
 a. are not influenced by birth order.
 b. can be influenced by their birth order.
 c. depend on the size of people's families.

B. *Listen to the conversation again. Fill in the chart.*

Person	Birth Order	Do the Character and the Description Match?
Mark's Brother		yes
Jeanne		
Mark		
Charles		

 SAY IT CLEARLY!

Primary and Secondary Word Stress

As you learned in Unit 5, compound nouns and adjectives have one syllable with primary stress and one syllable with secondary stress. Most English words of three or more syllables have one syllable with primary stress and one with secondary stress.

psychologists   personality

EXERCISE 10: *You Try It!*

A. *Listen to the words. Double underline the syllable with primary stress. Underline the syllable with secondary stress.*

humiliating   understanding   everybody   recognizing   paragraph

B. *Work with a partner. Take turns saying the words aloud.*

READ ABOUT IT!

Recognizing Generalizations

When we have a certain amount of information about a subject and want to make a broad statement about that subject, we may generalize. Generalizing allows us to extend or broaden information we have in order to make statements about what we don't know.

Bill is a thinker, not a doer.
Bill thought about his decision all day yesterday.
Personality tests are not very useful.
Question three of this test is confusing.

Which sentences are generalizations?

Are You an Idea Person or a Feeling Person?

by Debra M. Hall

This test will reveal if you are an idea person, almost always rational, or a feeling person, creative and spontaneous. By answering the questions, you'll find out something fascinating about yourself.

1. Which of the following describes you?
   a. A hard worker, intelligent and ambitious.
   b. Talented, good-looking, and with a great personality.
   c. Humorous, lucky, a team player.

2. What do you do when you run into a problem?
   a. Imagine how your close friends might resolve it.
   b. Review the facts, and then come up with a solution.
   c. Ask a family member to assist in solving the problem.

3. You enjoy exploring new ideas and
   a. comparing them to other ideas.
   b. analyzing them carefully.
   c. following up on them by adding some of your own thoughts.

4. Most of your family and friends believe that you are
   a. sensible and practical all the time.
   b. innovative and imaginative.
   c. a daydreamer.

5. You are most relaxed when you
   a. write essays and poems.
   b. draw pictures or go through art books.
   c. listen to music.

6. When faced with a number of tasks, you would
   a. do the work right away.
   b. put the work off for later, much later.
   c. work a little now, rest a bit, and finish later.

7. Video games are
   a. easier to play than computer games.
   b. better than board games such as chess.
   c. best suited for an arcade.

8. Most people would describe you as
   a. unable to make decisions.
   b. obstinate.
   c. in control at all times.

9. When dealing with instructions, you think the instructions
   a. should always be followed.
   b. should be ignored.
   c. should be considered somewhat.

10. When meeting people, you have a tendency to
    a. open up to them on the spot.
    b. hold back with them.
    c. be polite, reserving judgment until you get to know the people.

Analysis:
Use the grid to calculate your score.

Answer	1	2	3	4	5	6	7	8	9	10
a.	10	4	7	10	7	10	4	4	10	4
b.	7	10	10	7	4	7	7	7	4	7
c.	4	7	4	4	10	4	10	10	7	10

UP TO 59 POINTS: You are a feeling person. Your heart directs you in most of the decisions you make. You have a thinking style that is spatial, random, creative, and simultaneous. You prefer open-ended questions. You like manipulating objects, and prefer uncertain information. You use the right side of your brain most of the time. You are subjective. You enjoy music, video games, art, and geometrical puzzles. Your emotions are rather negative, but you are free with your feelings.

60 TO 80 POINTS: You are a straddler—you share characteristics of feelers and thinkers. Depending on how high or low your score is, you lean toward being more of a feeling person or a thinking person. As a straddler, you use both the right and left sides of your brain. Fusing ideas and feelings together, you are a well-adjusted person because you take the best of both halves. As a straddler, you enjoy singing, computer special effects seen in films, problem solving, and poetry. You are considered intuitive.

81 POINTS OR HIGHER: You are a thinker. You use the left side of your brain most of the time. You are a person full of wonderful, innovative ideas that are based on facts and other credible information. Your thinking style is verbal, orderly, and always in sequence. You are objective and enjoy reading, writing, and the intricacies of computer programming. While the feeling person is somewhat quiet, you enjoy talking! You are very rational, and have a tendency to really look at differences, see causes and effects, and have a preference for hierarchial set-ups. You are basically a planned and structured person.

Whether you lean to the left or the right, or are a thinker or a feeling person, remember—one is not better than another. The purpose of this test is to offer us some insight into your personality. After all, all of us enjoy finding out more about ourselves.

 EXERCISE 11: *Generally Speaking, ...*

What kinds of generalizations did the author make in the analysis? What did she probably base those generalizations on? Discuss your answer with a partner.

DISCUSSION

1. Are generalizations useful? When are generalizations harmful?

2. Why do people generalize?

3. Has anyone ever generalized unfairly about you? Have you ever made any unfair generalizations?

SPEAK OUT!

Giving Emphasis

When you want to stress a certain point in a conversation, you can use emphatic **do.** What other ways can you use to stress certain points?

Stating Generalizations

When we make generalizations, we introduce them with expressions that identify them as generalizations.

In general, ...	Generally speaking, ...
For the most part, ...	Everybody knows that. . . .

What other expressions can you think of to introduce generalizations?

 EXERCISE 12: *Is It Really You?*

*How accurate do you think the description the article provided of your personality is? Why? Discuss your reaction with two or three students. Use emphatic **do** to give emphasis to points you think are most important, and use appropriate language to express doubt and uncertainty.*

 WRITE ABOUT IT!

Introductory Paragraphs and Thesis Statements

The introductory paragraph of a multi-paragraph composition is usually ordered from general to specific. The first sentences give a broad idea of the topic and why it is important. The last sentence of the introduction makes a specific statement about what the body paragraph(s) will be about. This sentence is called a thesis statement. In longer articles, the writer sometimes divides the introduction into several paragraphs. Look at ''Personality's Part and Parcel'' on pages 88 and 89. How many paragraphs does the introduction have? What is the thesis statement?

 EXERCISE 13: *Writing Thesis Statements*

Read the introductory paragraph. Write an appropriate thesis statement on a sheet of paper.

1. Everybody has a preferred thinking style. Some people are highly creative and emotional. Others are more logical and rational.
2. Some people try to divide people into groups. For example, they divide them into groups of thinkers and feelers or thinkers and doers. In my opinion, there is a better way to divide people into groups.

 EXERCISE 14: *I Owe It All to You!*

Think of a person who has been an important influence in your life. How did he/she influence you? Develop a multi-paragraph narrative about the person you chose. Remember to introduce, support, and wrap up your topic. Make sure your introductory paragraph has a good thesis statement.

THINK ABOUT IT!

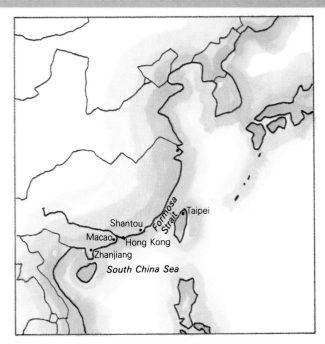

A. When Lin meets someone new who asks her where she's from, she says, "I'm from Hong Kong—it's a small island off the coast of China," because many people do not know exactly where Hong Kong is located. Has the same thing happened to you when you talk about your country, your hometown, or a place you have visited?

B. When do you use maps? What do you use them for? Where can you find them? How many different kinds of maps can you name? Make a list.

TALK IT OVER!

A. How many countries do you think there are in the world? Label as many as you can on the map.

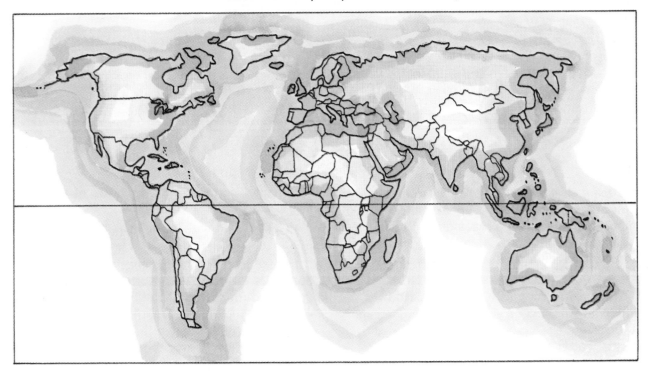

B. Compare your finished map with a partner's. Who labeled the most countries? Were some countries easier to remember than others? Why? Did you remember more countries in some geographical areas and not in others? Why do you think this was so?

READ ABOUT IT!

Getting Information from Maps

Getting information from maps is an important skill when reading. Understanding even a simple line map can clarify a text. However, there are many different kinds of maps, and different mapmakers can draw the same places in many ways. Look at the maps in the article. Who drew the maps? What are the differences between the maps? Why do you think that they are different? Would you draw the world the same as these map designers have done? Why or why not? If not, how would you draw the world?

Figuring Out the Intended Audience

Writers usually write with certain audiences in mind, and shape the article according to the interests and previous knowledge of those readers. For example, if the intended audience of an article on geography is tourists, the article will probably not be very technical or contain many specialized terms. However, an article on geography for an international journal for professional geographers would probably contain a great deal of highly technical information and specialized terms. As you read the article, try to figure out the audience the author probably had in mind.

Place Maps
by Cheryl Simon

Europe's on top of the world. Or, to be more precise, it dominates the upper middle. A set of more than 4,000 world maps drawn by first-year college students from 54 countries reveals that
5 most of the students see the world as Eurocentric.

Geographer Thomas F. Saarinen asked students who had taken at least one geography course to draw a world map in 30 minutes. He
10 found that even in countries such as Hong Kong, Singapore and Thailand, most students visualize Europe in the middle, although that view places their own countries on the map's edge. Saarinen believes that the Eurocentric
15 biases in the maps occur because one style of world map, the Mercator projection, has been

commonly used since the discovery of the New World.

Most Australian students sketched Sinocentric maps, with Australia and Asia in the center; 20 some featured Australia in the top-middle portion of the map, with North America "upside down" on the lower left. Although most North American students drew Eurocentric maps, the further west they lived in the United States and 25 Canada, the more likely they were to place the Americas in the center.

Large countries of continental dimensions such as the United States, the Soviet Union, India and Brazil appear on many of the maps. 30 So do prominent European nations such as France and Great Britain, as well as those with distinctive shapes, such as Italy or Chile. But small or landlocked nations are often nowhere 35 to be seen.

Researchers anticipated some of the results because of the effects of language, trade patterns and the lingering influences of colonialism. Saarinen expected, however, that 40 the students would exaggerate the size of their home continent. Instead, they consistently portrayed Europe as proportionately larger and underestimated Africa.

Although students from the United States 45 ranked with the world average in the number of countries they labeled—about 30 —they fared worse than average when it came to placing them correctly. Students from Hungary and the Soviet Union, where the educational systems stress geography, produced many of the best 50 maps.

Saarinen is coding the information and will analyze it in terms of culture, location and size of the portrayed image relative to a geographical feature's true proportions. Through the project, 55 sponsored by the International Geographical Union, Saarinen hopes to reveal regional distortions. "If there is to be peace, we need a shared world image of some sort," Saarinen says. "We have to let students know it's OK if 60 someone somewhere else has a different view— that this is a natural outcome of one's position on earth."

EXERCISE 1: *Meaning from Context*

A. *Use your knowledge of word parts and the context to figure out the meaning of the word. Write the definition on a sheet of paper.*

1. prominent *(line 31)*
2. distinctive *(line 33)*
3. landlocked *(line 34)*
4. anticipate *(line 36)*
5. exaggerate *(line 40)*
6. underestimate *(line 43)*

B. *Find a synonym for the word in the article. Write the synonym on the line.*

1. draw _____
2. see _____
3. show _____
4. size _____

EXERCISE 2: *Check the Facts!*

*Circle **T** if the statement is true. Circle **F** if the statement is false.*

T F **1.** Hungarian students were better than U.S. students in placing countries when they drew maps.

T F **2.** Most students could name about fifty countries.

T F **3.** The experiment had 54,000 participants.

T F **4.** Students from New York were more likely to put the U.S. in the middle of the map than students from California.

T F **5.** Saarinen believes that the world can be depicted in the same way by everyone.

EXERCISE 3: *Who Is It For?*

A. *Who did you think the article was intended for? Circle the answer or answers.*

students	teachers	mapmakers	geologists
parents	psychologists	tourists	government officials

B. *Work with a partner. Decide whether the article is very technical. Why or why not? How might the article be different if it were intended for the audiences you did NOT circle?*

EXERCISE 4: *Mapmakers*

Use the information in the article to figure out how the people in the questions would draw maps.

1. Where might someone from Spain place Europe on a map? Would the continent be large or small?
2. Would someone from the southern tip of Argentina place his or her country at the top or at the bottom of a map?
3. Would people be more likely to include Morocco or Rwanda on a map? Why?

 WORD FOR WORD!

Why is Snoopy confused? Do you ever feel confused by a map? What geographic features can be marked on a map? Work with a partner and make a list of all the various ways geographic features can be marked on a map.

PEANUTS reprinted by permission of UFS, Inc.

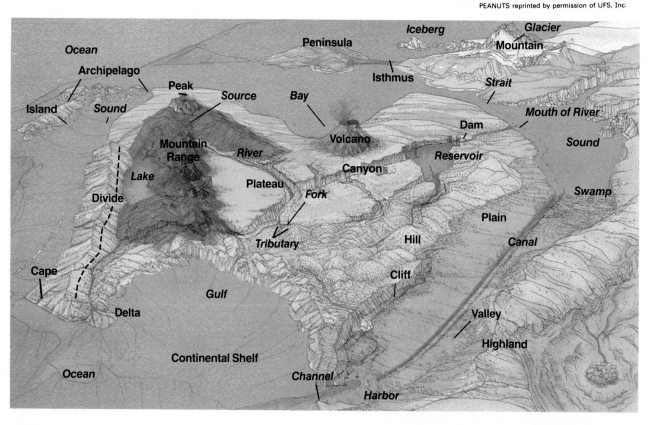

EXERCISE 5: *Land's Sake!*

Use the map on page 102 to figure out the meaning of each
geographical term in column 1. Write the letter on the line.

_____ **1.** harbor	**a.** an enclosed area of water safe for ships to stay in
_____ **2.** swamp	**b.** a tall wall of rock or earth
_____ **3.** canal	**c.** part of an ocean or lake that extends into the land
_____ **4.** canyon	**d.** a waterway dug across land
_____ **5.** cliff	**e.** a wide, flat area of land
_____ **6.** archipelago	**f.** a triangular-shaped deposit of earth and sand that builds up where some rivers empty into a lake or a sea
_____ **7.** channel	
_____ **8.** valley	**g.** low land between two mountains or hills
_____ **9.** bay	**h.** a long, narrow body of water that joins two larger bodies of water
_____ **10.** peninsula	
_____ **11.** delta	**i.** a long, narrow cut in the land with tall rock walls made by a river
_____ **12.** island	
	j. an area of low-lying land where water collects
	k. a group of islands
	l. a piece of land that extends from the mainland into the water
	m. a piece of land completely surrounded by water

EXERCISE 6: *Land, Ho!*

Think of a country or place familiar to you and map out its geography on
a sheet of paper. Then work with a partner. Use your map to give your
partner a tour, pointing out the most important geographic features.
Would your partner like to live or visit there? Why or why not?

SPEAK OUT!

Conceding a Point

We often have strong viewpoints about certain subjects and may
discuss them with other people who have equally strong viewpoints.
During a discussion, we may find that we disagree. However, we may
become convinced of someone else's viewpoint concerning one part of
an argument, and agree only on that point.

Disagreeing Politely

If we cannot agree, but want to avoid an argument, we may politely
disagree, or we may "agree to disagree." We decide that we are
unable to settle our differences and decide to continue discussing other
points or end the conversation. Underline the language the speakers in
the conversation use to concede a point, to disagree politely, and to
agree to disagree.

JAVIER: Well, our assignment was to discuss maps and reality. I've
checked ten atlases, and they all give clear pictures of the world and
lots of facts.

HIROKO: I agree to a certain extent, but some people would say that
sometimes information is missing from maps.

JAVIER: Well, you may be right. They can't show everything.

ANDREW: What about aerial maps? They show the earth exactly as it is.

HIROKO: Not always. You see, light and atmosphere can make objects look different when in fact they are the same. The angle of the sun can make a difference, too. If the sun is very low, long shadows will cover up small features. If the sun is high and bright, the shadow of the plane can interfere.

ANDREW: Are you trying to say that maps aren't accurate?

HIROKO: I'm only saying that we have to evaluate the information on a map carefully. Look at this one. It shows the route of an oil pipeline from Prudhoe Bay to Port Valdez in Alaska.

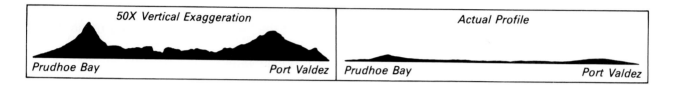

ANDREW: Wow! Through all those mountains!

HIROKO: Yes, it *was* difficult to build it, but look. It says "fifty times vertical exaggeration," so that means it would really look like this.

JAVIER: I suppose you're right. The first map is misleading—but that's just one map. But I still think that most maps are accurate.

HIROKO: Let's just say that we have to evaluate maps to make sure we're not being misled.

JAVIER: I guess I can live with that.

ANDREW: Well, I agree more with Hiroko. I think that many times maps give wrong impressions. For example, on this map, Greenland looks much bigger than on this map. Look.

HIROKO: Right. That's what I'm trying to say. The first map is an example of the Mercator projection, which makes the North and South Poles look much bigger than they really are. The other map shows the land masses in their correct relative sizes.

JAVIER: Look, Hiroko, it seems to me that you think all maps are wrong!

HIROKO: OK, OK. Let's just agree to disagree!

EXERCISE 7: *City Maps*

Work with two other students. Your city government has asked you to serve on a committee to decide whether city signs and maps should be written in the languages tourists in the city speak. The percentage of visitors who speak each language is in the chart. Recommend which languages, if any, should be used in the maps and signs. Keep in mind the cost of making signs and maps, and the importance of tourism to the city. Use language for conceding a point and disagreeing politely. Agree to disagree if necessary.

Spanish	32%
Japanese	24%
Korean	16%
French	12%
Polish	10%
Arabic	6%

FIGURE IT OUT!

A. *Indefinite and Definite Articles*

We use the indefinite and definite articles **a/an** and **the** differently with nouns depending on whether they are singular or plural, specific or nonspecific, and mass (such as **land**) or count (such as **mountain**).

We use the indefinite article **a/an** when we talk about nonspecific singular count nouns. With nonspecific plural count nouns, we use no article.

> A: I'd like **a map** of Coral Island, please.
> B: Here you are.
> A: This map is a little hard to read. I like **clear, detailed maps.** Do you have **a better map?**

We use the definite article **the** with specific singular and plural count nouns.

> B: Yes, this map is larger and has more detail. **The free maps** aren't as clear because they're not in color. Also, they don't show all **the side streets. The color maps** are fifteen dollars. They're much more complete, and they're easier to use.
> A: How much is **the map** on the wall?
> B: **The map** on the wall is a special map of the coral reefs. It shows all **the best places** to see the reefs. It also contains information on diving and snorkeling. It costs thirty-two dollars.
> A: I see. I'll take a copy of **the fifteen dollar map,** please.

With nonspecific mass nouns we use no article. With specific mass nouns we use **the.**

> A: By the way, I need to buy **food.** Are grocery stores on Coral Island open on Sundays?
> B: Well, the store in Central Square is open until three. But **the food** there is very expensive. You probably could get a better meal in a restaurant for the same price.

A. *When do we use **a/an** and **the**? Read the examples again and organize the information in the chart. Write **a/an** or **the**. If no article is necessary, write **X**.*

	Count Nouns		Mass Nouns
	Singular	Plural	
Specific	the		
Nonspecific			

B. *Write **a/an** or **the** on the line as necessary. If no word is necessary, write **X**.*

1. _____ cartographer draws _____ maps.

2. _____ cartographer who drew _____ maps in this atlas did a good job.

3. _____ map of South America in this atlas is gorgeous.

4. I sketched _____ map at the beginning of this unit.

5. This encyclopedia contains _____ information you want.

6. _____ atlas on the table contains _____ information on climate, geology, and land use.

B. The Definite Article with Place Names

In general, we do not use **the** before most place names.

There are some exceptions to this rule.

> A: Is our hotel on **Coral Island** very nice?
> B: Yes, it's a block from **Central Square,** which is the nicest part of town. It's right here on the map where **King Street** meets **Bridgeforth Avenue.**

Streets	Fifth Avenue	The Avenue of the Americas
Towns	Miami	The City of Miami *(formal)*
States and Provinces	California Alberta	The State of California *(formal)*
Countries	Spain, England	The United States The Sudan
Mountains	Mount Everest *(individual mountains)*	The Andes, The Rocky Mountains *(mountain ranges)*
Islands	Jamaica Puerto Rico *(individual islands)*	The Philippines The Hawaiian Islands *(archipelagos)*
Oceans		The Atlantic Ocean
Lakes	Lake Michigan	The Great Salt Lake
Rivers		The Amazon The Mississippi
Canals		The Panama Canal The Suez Canal
Deserts		The Sahara

EXERCISE 9: *I'd Love to Visit. . . .*

A. *Write **the** on the line when necessary. If **the** is not necessary, write **X** on the line. As you read, try to figure out which country the text is about.*

I'd love to visit a beautiful country in **(1)** _____ Africa, about four thousand feet (1200 meters) above sea level. It is inland, about eight hundred miles (1300 kilometers) from **(2)** _____ Indian Ocean. However, it borders on **(3)** _____ Lake Victoria, which it shares with two other countries, **(4)** _____ Kenya and Tanzania. **(5)** _____ Lake Victoria is the source of **(6)** _____ Nile River, which flows north through **(7)** _____ Sudan and **(8)** _____ Egypt to **(9)** _____ Mediterranean Sea. On the southwest border with **(10)** _____ Rwanda-Burundi are **(11)** _____ Mountains of the Moon.

B. *Could you figure out the country? Check your answer on page 110.*

C. *Write a similar paragraph about a place you'd love to visit. Do not write the country's name. Show your paragraph to a partner. Can your partner figure out which country you wrote about?*

LISTEN TO THIS!

When do you give directions? When do you ask for directions? Sometimes people ask for directions, but then get more confused after hearing them! Has this ever happened to you?

EXERCISE 10: *You Can't Miss It!*

A. *Listen to the conversations and circle the answers.*

1. What road does Anna have to take?
Road 123   Road 103   Road 133

2. Has Anna ever been to this place before?
yes   no

3. What's Pat's address?
5341 Royal   5431 Royal   5134 Royal

B. *Listen to the conversation again. Trace the route on the map.*

C. *Work with a partner. You are at Pat's house and one of you wants directions to the golf course. Take turns asking for and giving directions.*

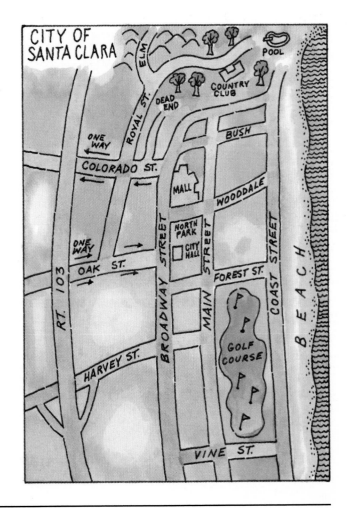

SAY IT CLEARLY!

Sentence Stress

The words in every sentence contain a number of stressed and unstressed syllables. Normally, one of these stressed syllables carries the primary stress of the sentence. Usually, this is the last stressed syllable.

> Patricia often travels **abroad.** Jim likes to stay at home and **read.**

If we want to emphasize a contrast, a syllable in another word can be stressed. For example, if we want to clarify something that we didn't hear very well, we can use sentence stress to ask about and state the word we are clarifying. If we are disagreeing with someone, we can stress the words we are insisting upon as correct.

> A: **Where** did John go?
> B: I said that he went **up north.**
> A: Oh, I thought that you said that he went **abroad.**
> B: John **never** travels abroad.
> A: Yes, he **does.** He goes abroad every **year.** Last year he went to **Korea.**

Which words were stressed in order to clarify? Which words were being stressed in a disagreement?

EXERCISE 11: *What I Mean Is. . . .*

Listen to the conversations. Write the word with sentence stress on the line.

1. Conversation 1: _____
2. Conversation 2: _____
3. Conversation 3: _____

EXERCISE 12: *What I Said Was. . . .*

A. *Read the conversations. Which words do you think will have sentence stress? Underline a word or words in each of the sentences in **dark type.***

1. A: The Great Lakes are very polluted.
   B: **The Great Lakes were very polluted.**
2. C: There are some people who think that the earth is flat.
   D: **Nobody believes the earth is flat!**
3. E: Maps are boring.
   F: **No, they're fascinating!**

B. *Work with a partner. Listen to the conversations and then take turns saying them aloud.*

READ ABOUT IT!

Maps and Charts

Look at the map and the statistics chart. What information does each one contain?

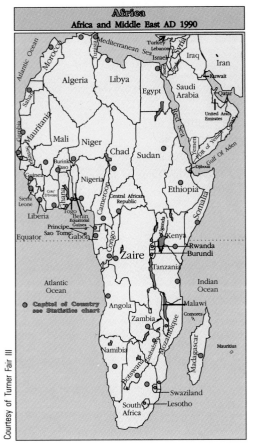

Courtesy of Turner Fair III

Country	Capitol	Population 1981 in Millions	Area 1000 Sq. Miles	Year of Colonial Independence
Algeria	Algiers	19.6	919.7	1962
Angola	Luanda	7.8	481.5	1975
Benin	Porto Novo	3.6	43.6	1960
Botswana	Gabarone	0.9	231.7	1966
Bunnka Faso	Ouagadougou	6.3	105.8	1960
Burundi	Bujumbura	4.2	10.8	1962
Cameroon	Yaounde'	8.2	183.4	1960
Cape Verde	Pria	0.3	1.5	1975
Central African Republic	Bangui	2.4	240.5	1960
Chad	N'djamena	4.5	495.8	1960
Comoros	Moroni	0.4	0.8	1975
Congo	Brazzaville	1.7	132.0	1960
Djibouti	Djibouti	0.4	8.5	1977
Egypt	Cairo	43.3	386.5	1922
Equatorial Guinea	Malabo	0.3	10.8	1968
Ethiopia	Addis Ababa	31.8	471.8	not a colony
Gabon	Libreville	0.7	103.5	1960
Gambia, The	Banjul	0.6	4.2	1965
Ghana	Accra	11.8	92.3	1957
Guinea	Conkary	5.6	95.0	1958
Guinea-Bissau	Bissau	0.8	13.9	1974
Ivory Coast	Yamoussoukro	8.5	124.3	1960
Kenya	Nairobi	17.4	225.1	1963
Lesotho	Maseru	1.4	11.6	1966
Liberia	Monrovia	1.9	42.9	1847

The Continent

Area = 11,700,000 square miles (30,300,000 square kilometers)

Second in size to Asia

Length (north to south) = 5000 miles
From Ras ben Sekka, Tunisia to Cape Agulhas, South Africa

Width (east to west) = 4600 miles
From Ras Hafun, Somalia to Cape Verde, Senegal

Highest Point = Mt. Kilamanjaro 19,340 feet

Coast line = 18,950 miles

Lowest Point = Lake Assal 509 feet below sea level

Population = 350,000,000, 10% of the world

Great Rift Valley of Africa (in east) is known for wealth of archaeological finds (Ethiopia, Somalia, Kenya, Tanzania).

map and chart showing one Afrocentric view of the world

EXERCISE 13: It's on the Map!

What information from the chart could a mapmaker include on the map? Why do you think the mapmaker chose to draw the map this way?

SPEAK OUT!

Expressing Lack of Understanding

With maps, as well as other things, we often find ourselves confused. As a result, we sometimes express our confusion and bewilderment. Look at the conversation. How do the people express their lack of understanding? Underline the words and expressions.

A: I'm so terrible with maps. I really don't have a clue how to use them.

B: Well, I'm pretty good at maps and directions, but don't ask me to help anyone with homework! Math, especially. Math is Greek to me!

A: You know, that's interesting, because I'm pretty sharp at math, but I find literature hard. Analyzing a literary text is completely beyond me.

EXERCISE 14: *Strengths and Weaknesses*

List five things you feel you do well, and five things you feel you lack understanding about. Then, work with a partner and discuss your lists. Are you good at the same things? Are you bewildered by the same things? Can you help each other out in those areas you feel you lack understanding in?

WRITE ABOUT IT!

Transitions Between Paragraphs

In Unit 6 you learned that we use transitional devices to relate sentences to each other within a paragraph. When writing a multi-paragraph composition, we use transitional sentences to connect those paragraphs together. For example, in a composition in which we present different points of view, we can use transitional words and expressions that show comparison and contrast to link the ideas in different paragraphs together. Look at the model.

(title) ∼∼∼∼∼∼∼∼∼∼∼∼∼∼∼∼∼∼∼∼∼∼∼∼∼∼∼∼∼∼

The decision to design maps with northern or southern orientation is an important question. ∼∼∼∼∼∼∼∼∼∼∼∼∼∼∼∼∼∼∼∼∼
∼∼∼∼∼∼∼∼∼∼∼∼∼∼∼∼∼∼∼∼∼∼∼∼∼∼∼∼∼∼∼∼∼∼∼∼∼∼∼
∼∼∼∼∼∼∼∼∼∼∼∼∼∼∼∼∼∼∼∼∼∼∼∼∼∼∼∼∼∼∼∼∼∼∼∼∼∼∼

There are several arguments in favor of putting South at the top of maps. ∼∼∼∼∼∼∼∼∼∼∼∼∼∼∼∼∼∼∼∼∼∼∼∼∼∼∼∼
∼∼∼∼∼∼∼∼∼∼∼∼∼∼∼∼∼∼∼∼∼∼∼∼∼∼∼∼∼∼∼∼∼∼∼∼∼∼∼
∼∼∼∼∼∼∼∼∼∼∼∼∼∼∼∼∼∼∼∼∼∼∼∼∼∼∼∼∼∼∼∼∼∼∼∼∼∼∼

However, there are several disadvantages also. ∼∼∼∼∼∼∼∼∼∼∼∼∼
∼∼∼∼∼∼∼∼∼∼∼∼∼∼∼∼∼∼∼∼∼∼∼∼∼∼∼∼∼∼∼∼∼∼∼∼∼∼∼
∼∼∼∼∼∼∼∼∼∼∼∼∼∼∼∼∼∼∼∼∼∼∼∼∼∼∼∼∼∼∼∼∼∼∼∼∼∼∼

These disadvantages strengthen the reasoning of those designers who favor putting North at the top of maps. ∼∼∼∼∼∼∼∼∼∼∼∼
∼∼∼∼∼∼∼∼∼∼∼∼∼∼∼∼∼∼∼∼∼∼∼∼∼∼∼∼∼∼∼∼∼∼∼∼∼∼∼
∼∼∼∼∼∼∼∼∼∼∼∼∼∼∼∼∼∼∼∼∼∼∼∼∼∼∼∼∼∼∼∼∼∼∼∼∼∼∼

In conclusion, as the advantages of northern orientation in map design outweigh those of southern orientation, it is in the best interest of map designers and users to continue to see North at the top of their maps. ∼∼∼∼∼∼∼∼∼∼∼∼∼∼∼∼∼∼∼∼∼∼
∼∼∼∼∼∼∼∼∼∼∼∼∼∼∼∼∼∼∼∼∼∼∼∼∼∼∼∼∼∼∼∼∼∼∼∼∼∼∼
∼∼∼∼∼∼∼∼∼∼∼∼∼∼∼∼∼∼∼∼∼∼∼∼∼∼∼∼∼∼∼∼∼∼∼∼∼∼∼

EXERCISE 15: *In Comparison*

You are an employee of a map company. Your boss has asked you for a report comparing maps on paper to maps on globes. Write a multi-paragraph report considering the different sides to the question. Follow the model and the steps of the writing process.

 THINK ABOUT IT!

A. What is your idea of a great vacation? Would you rather travel or stay at home? stay in your own country or visit another? relax and do nothing or be busy at every moment?

B. What words do you associate with **adventure?** Fill in the word map with your ideas. Then compare your map with a partner's.

adventure

 TALK IT OVER!

A. Many people are attracted to the idea of adventure vacations. This type of vacation, growing in popularity around the world, provides ordinary people with the opportunity to experience strong emotions, thrills, and challenges normally reserved for the adventurous few. Look at the examples of types of adventure vacations. What kinds of activities are involved in each one? Which ones appeal to you? Share your ideas with a partner.

a cave-exploring trip
a dinosaur dig
a photographic safari
a white-water rafting trip

a mountain-climbing trip
a cowboy-style cattle drive
a war games camp
a horseback tour of a country

B. How dangerous do you think these adventure vacations are? Rank them in order of danger from **1** for the most dangerous to **8** for the least dangerous. Do you and your partner agree on your rankings?

READ ABOUT IT!

Recognizing Comparisons and Contrasts

Writers often point out similarities and differences between two objects, people, or ideas. Recognizing comparisons and contrasts enables the reader to relate something new to something familiar and form a mental picture of the subject. As you read the article "Junko Tabei: Mountain Climber," observe how the author makes comparisons and contrasts. Remember that the comparisons may be **explicit** (stated in the text) or **implicit** (implied in the text).

Junko Tabei: Mountain Climber
by Jerdine Nolen-Harold

Imagine that you are the leader of a mountain-climbing expedition that will take you to the top of the world—the peak of Mt. Everest, 8,848 meters (29,030 feet) high. Thin air, freezing winds, and numbingly cold temperatures stand between you and
5 your goal. You're in your tent in the frigid cold when an avalanche strikes. You are buried under a block of ice. You cannot move. You can barely breathe. What do you think about?

For Junko Tabei, the first woman to climb Mt. Everest, it was the family she had left behind in Japan. Her thoughts went to her
10 three-year-old daughter. She wondered how her little girl would get along without her mother. Tabei then lost consciousness for about six minutes, while her Sherpa guide dug her out.

With no intention of giving up, she continued climbing, despite the injuries she had received in the avalanche. It would take all of
15 the tenacity, strength, and will she could summon to become the first woman to conquer Mt. Everest. She remembers the feeling when she reached the summit. "There was no enjoyment, just relief. I was very, very happy that I didn't have to climb anymore."

Mt. Everest is said to be unforgiving. Temperatures can plunge
20 to well below freezing. The mountain's extreme steepness, together with its strong winds, thin air, and deep crevasses make the climb extremely dangerous. Climbers must be experienced mountaineers in top physical condition. As they reach higher altitudes, they have to stop to let their bodies adjust to the lack
25 of oxygen. In the ascent, the climbers have to carry thousands of pounds of equipment with them. Over sixty-nine people have died while trying to reach the top. Eleven expeditions had tried and failed to reach the top before Sir Edmund Hillary and Tenzing Norgay, a Sherpa tribesman, did so on May 10, 1953. Tabei's
30 expedition included fifteen Japanese women and over fifteen tons of supplies and equipment (including tents, sleeping bags, food, stoves, fuel, clothing, climbing tools, and oxygen). Like climbers who had gone before them, they established a series of base camps up the side of the mountain. Climbers worked in groups
35 moving equipment up the mountain from one camp to the next, returning at night to the lower camp for a day of rest at a warmer altitude.

Climbing Mt. Everest takes two months or more, but months or even years of preparation are required before the climb begins.

40 Supplies, transportation to Katmandu, Nepal, salaries for Sherpa guides, and fees charged by the Nepalese government all must be paid for. For Tabei, the preparations were almost as daunting as the climb. While seeking funding for her expedition, Tabei approached a large corporation, which told her that it was

45 impossible for a woman to climb Mt. Everest and that she ought to go home and take care of her baby! This made Tabei even more determined, and she began to raise the money she needed for the trip by giving piano lessons in her home. Later she got additional funding from a television network to help pay for her

50 fifteen-woman expedition.

Tabei was thirty-five years old when she climbed Mt. Everest. Since then, the 4'11" (1.49 meters) tall woman has become the first female to prevail over the highest mountains on six of the world's seven continents, including Mt. Blanc in Europe, Mt.

55 Kilimanjaro in Africa, Mt. Aconcagua in South America, Mt. McKinley in North America, and Mt. Vinson Massif in Antarctica. To reach her goal of covering all seven continents, she is awaiting permission from the Indonesian government to climb Mt. Jaya. Tabei's goal after that is to climb the highest mountain in each

60 country in the world. She says that she plans to finish in 2020, when she is eighty years old.

Tabei became interested in mountaineering at an early age. When she was ten years old, she climbed a small mountain while on a class field trip. That experience changed her life forever—

65 she realized that there were many places in the world that she knew nothing about. Her climbing has taken her to places in the world which many people only dream about, or which they may not have even heard of!

Junko Tabei is living the kind of life she wants. She certainly is

70 not living the life of a typical housewife, and she thinks of herself as a career woman. Since her climb, she has become famous. She has received awards and congratulations from the prime minister of Japan and the king of Nepal, and other heads of state. She gives interviews, lectures at universities, and appears on TV

75 talk shows. She makes enough money from her lectures and appearances to pay for her expeditions—she no longer has to depend on corporate sponsors. Nevertheless, she is very devoted to her family, getting up early to give her children breakfast and leaving supper on the stove for her family while she is appearing

80 on TV. Tabei therefore feels that she uses her time much better as a career woman than she would as a full-time housewife, and hopes that she will leave behind an interesting personal history.

DISCUSSION

1. Why do people want to put their lives in danger to climb mountains?

2. Mt. Everest is said to be the home of the Abominable Snowman, a legendary ape-like creature. Do you believe that such a being can exist? Why or why not?

3. Have you ever climbed a mountain? gone hiking in the hills? Share your experience.

EXERCISE 1: *Meaning from Context*

Match the words in column 1 with the meanings in column 2. Write the letter on the line.

_____ **1.** expedition *(lines 2, 27, 30, 43, 50, 76)*

_____ **2.** barely *(line 7)*

_____ **3.** tenacity *(line 15)*

_____ **4.** summon *(line 15)*

_____ **5.** plunge *(line 19)*

_____ **6.** daunting *(line 42)*

_____ **7.** funding *(lines 43, 49)*

_____ **8.** no longer *(line 76)*

a. not anymore, not now
b. money for expenses
c. trip, travel
d. presenting a challenge
e. just a little
f. fascinating
g. determination
h. fall
i. call up, collect

EXERCISE 2: *Implicit or Explicit?*

The chart lists some of the items the author compares, implicitly or explicitly, in the article. Analyze the comparisons and complete the chart. Label each comparison as **I** *for implicit or* **E** *for explicit.*

The author compares:	with:	Comparison Type:
1. Tabei's height		
2. raising money by giving piano lessons		
3. Tabei's life at home with her family		
4. difficulty of the climb		

EXERCISE 3: *The Adventures of Junko Tabei*

Put the events in Junko Tabei's life in chronological order. Number the events from **1** *(first) to* **6** *(last).*

_____ **a.** Tabei reached the top of Mt. Everest.

_____ **b.** Tabei climbed her first mountain.

_____ **c.** Tabei gave piano lessons to earn money.

_____ **d.** Tabei reached her fifty-second birthday.

_____ **e.** Tabei climbed Mt. Kilimanjaro.

_____ **f.** Tabei began preparing to climb Mt. Everest.

WORD FOR WORD!

Plays on Words

A play on words occurs when a word used in a sentence has two meanings: one which makes sense in the sentence, and another which relates to the topic of the sentence. Look at the examples.

Junko Tabei is in her peak years as a climber.
    (**peak** means "best" and also means "mountain top")
The fireworks business is booming.
    (**boom** means "increase" and also means "explode")

A play on words may also be based on homonyms—words spelled differently that sound alike.

What's black and white and read all over? A newspaper.
    (**read** sounds the same as **red**, the color)

 ## EXERCISE 4: *Double Play*

Underline the word or words in the sentences that are being "played on." Then identify the two meanings of the word which make it a play on words.

1. For trash collectors, business is picking up.

2. Crossing Death Valley was the low point of my life!

3. Shall we have a salad? Yes, lettuce!

4. For crossword fans, life is a puzzle.

5. Ann's boyfriend rose to the occasion by bringing her one!

 # SPEAK OUT!

Expressing Feelings as a Listener

Active listeners in a conversation may express a number of different feelings as they listen. Expressing feelings like doubt, surprise, sympathy, and interest helps keep a conversation going and shows that the listener is involved in what the other speaker is saying.

EXERCISE 5: *Tell Me More!*

A. *With a partner, make a list of expressions you have learned that show feelings (uncertainty, surprise, enthusiasm, etc.). Share your list with the class.*

B. *In the conversation between Ross and Joan, how many kinds of feelings are expressed?*

ROSS: Hey, where'd you get that beautiful necklace?

JOAN: In the Philippines.

ROSS: The Philippines? What were you doing in the Philippines?

JOAN: Well . . . I was on an adventure vacation.

ROSS: You? No kidding! I didn't know that! What kind of adventure?

JOAN: Well, it was a scuba diving trip, actually, but . . . .

ROSS: Scuba diving? That's great! I had no idea you were a scuba diver.

JOAN: Well, that's the thing. I'm not really.

ROSS: But you just said . . .

JOAN: I know, I know. See, I was at this travel fair at school, and there was this diving company that was having a contest, see, and you had to guess how many pearls there were in this jar, and the person who guessed the closest won, and the prize was a diving trip to the Philippines, and, well, I won.

ROSS: I don't believe it! You *won* the whole trip?

JOAN: Well, yeah—the air fare and hotels and food.

ROSS: That's fantastic!

JOAN: Well, yeah—but there was one problem.

ROSS: What?

JOAN: I don't know how to dive.

ROSS: You're kidding!

JOAN: No, I'm not. I don't swim very well, and what's more I don't even like the water much. But I'd always wanted to visit the Philippines, so I went.

ROSS: That's great. So tell me about it.

JOAN: Well, we were there for ten days, which wasn't long enough, and we stayed on three islands: Luzon, Cebu and Bohol. We traveled around by bus and small plane and on boats called banquas, that are sort of like canoes.

ROSS: That's really neat. So did you go diving in all the places you visited?

JOAN: Well, there were twelve people on the trip who'd paid to go, and *they* went diving.

ROSS: What about you? You must have at least tried it!

JOAN: Oh yes, I tried, but things kept going wrong.

ROSS: Like what?

JOAN: Oh, you have to wear a lot of equipment, which is really heavy, and you have to practice in shallow water before you try the deeper water. But the waves were really high and they kept knocking me down and I couldn't get back up!

ROSS: Oh, that's awful.

JOAN: I did finally get out in the deep water, but what was even worse were the little biting fish you can't even see.

ROSS: That's really too bad. Did you have a good time at all?

JOAN: Oh absolutely! The Philippines is a beautiful country, and I spent most of my time relaxing on the beach and eating the great food.

ROSS: So you'd recommend that kind of vacation?

JOAN: Oh, for sure—for people who can dive!

EXERCISE 6: *What a Feeling!*

What expressions were used to communicate feelings? Fill in the chart with words and expressions for each category. Then compare your chart with a partner's.

Feelings	Expressions
1. enthusiasm	
2. disbelief	
3. interest	
4. sympathy	
5. certainty	

Building up to a Climax in a Narrative

One strategy speakers and writers often use to make a narrative or story more interesting is that of **building up to a climax.** Narrators gradually include descriptive details that increase the listener's or reader's anticipation before the most important or exciting part of the story.

 EXERCISE 7: *What a Story!*

A. *Where in the conversation does Joan build up to a climax? How does she do it? Support your answers with examples.*

B. *Work with a partner. Take turns telling a story to each other using one of the sentences as your story climax. Try to make your story as exciting as possible and gradually build up details to the climax. Your partner will express appropriate feelings about your story as you tell it.*

1. He crossed the finish line first!
2. It was the children next door!
3. Then I heard my name announced as the winner!
4. They were married and began their new life together.
5. I finally reached the door just as they were closing it!

 FIGURE IT OUT!

A. *Restrictive and Non-Restrictive Clauses*

1. As you learned in Unit 7, we use a restrictive clause to describe a noun and to give information essential to our understanding. We use a non-restrictive clause when we give additional, but not essential, information about a noun.

Restrictive:	Lucy is one of those people who always does something new and adventurous on her vacations.
Non-Restrictive:	Her last vacation, which she'd been planning for a long time, was a great success.

You also learned that we set off non-restrictive clauses with commas and that the restrictive/non-restrictive distinction sometimes influences meaning.

> The climbing ropes which were in poor condition were sent out to be repaired.
> The climbing ropes, which were in poor condition, were sent out to be repaired.

In which sentence were all the ropes sent out for repairs? only some of the ropes? How do you know?

EXERCISE 8: *Kon-Tiki*

Complete the sentences with relative pronouns. If no pronoun is needed, write **X**. *Add commas where necessary.*

Kon-Tiki is the name of a raft **(1.)** _____ was built by

Thor Heyerdahl in the 1940s. Heyerdahl wanted to prove that

people **(2.)** _____ came from South America could have

sailed to Polynesia hundreds of years before. To test his theory

Heyerdahl **(3.)** _____ was from Norway had a raft built in

Peru from trees and other materials **(4.)** _____ grew in

the area. He named the raft Kon-Tiki **(5.)** _____ was the

name of an ancient Inca god. In 1947, Heyerdahl and five others

set out from Callao, Peru **(6.)** _____ is on the western

coast of South America. The route **(7.)** _____ Heyerdahl

took did eventually take them to islands near Tahiti. He crossed

some 5000 miles (8000 km) of ocean and took 3 1/2 months.

Heyerdahl kept a detailed record of the trip **(8.)** _____

was later published. The Kon-Tiki is now on display in a museum

in Oslo, Norway.

2. Another difference between restrictive and non-restrictive clauses lies in the use of the relative pronouns.

> Few people **who** go on adventure vacations regret the experience.
> The people **that** sign up for adventure vacations want a physical and mental challenge.
> A vacation **which** provides such a challenge helps people find out more about themselves.
> The vacation **that** becomes a true learning experience is the most satisfying kind to have.
> Adventurous people, **who** may be of any age, find psychological satisfaction in their actions.
> This feeling of satisfaction, **which** may or may not last long, motivates these people to try for yet another adventure.

EXERCISE 9: *Sum It Up!*

Using the sentences in the box for reference, complete the chart summarizing the use of relative pronouns in restrictive and non-restrictive clauses.

Subject	Relative Pronouns: Restrictive	Relative Pronouns: Non-Restrictive
people	**who** or _____	_____
things	_____ or _____	_____

B. *Parenthetical Information*

A parenthetical expression such as **I suppose, I remember, we imagine,** etc., does not affect the form of the relative pronoun.

> Steve, who I remember was physically inactive back in school, went on a mountain-climbing expedition for his vacation.
> **(who** is the subject of **was)**

Parenthetical information is not limited to nonrestrictive relative clauses. There are many other ways of presenting separate, additional units of information. Punctuation plays an important part in the indication of these units, which may be set off by commas, parentheses, or dashes. However, in certain cases there may be no punctuation.

> Dr. Smith the explorer gave a lecture last night.
> Everything we need for our trip—food, equipment, and transportation—is ready.
> Our group leader sent ahead the Sherpa guide, in other words the most experienced climber in the group.
> This travel book contains some wonderful descriptions, particularly the ones of West Africa.
> The one sport Bob enjoys (sky diving) has allowed him to meet new people.
> She conquered Mt. Everest, 8,848 meters (29,030 feet) high.

 EXERCISE 10: *Parenthetically Speaking . . .*

Work with a partner. Express your feelings about the topics in the list. Make sentences with relative clauses and other types of parenthetical information.

1. people who won't try something new
2. people who break rules
3. activities that are physically dangerous
4. your own idea

 LISTEN TO THIS!

We all have favorite radio and TV announcers. What qualities distinguish them?

EXERCISE 11:
In the News

A. *Listen to three commentaries by different radio announcers. Which word best describes the tone of each commentary? Write the number of the commentary on the line.*

_____ **a.** serious _____ **b.** sarcastic _____ **c.** enthusiastic _____ **d.** disappointed

B. *Listen to the commentaries again. What kind of event is each announcer describing? Write the number on the line in the correct picture above.*

 SAY IT CLEARLY!

Intonation with Parenthetical Information

In spoken English, parenthetical information is set off by different intonation, voice intensity, and the use of pauses. Changing the intonation of a sentence can change its meaning. A restrictive clause tends to be stressed as part of the sentence, while a non-restrictive clause tends to be stressed as an independent unit. We also signal this separation by a slight drop in voice intensity and by pausing slightly at the commas.

> The guides who came with us were very experienced.
> The guides, who came with us, were very experienced.

EXERCISE 12: *The Ear for It*

A. *Listen to the sentences in the box on page 119. What changes in intonation, voice intensity, and pausing tell you the sentences have different meanings?*

B. *Now listen to three different sets of sentences. As you listen to each separate sentence, decide if the sentence contains a restrictive or non-restrictive clause. Write **R** (restrictive) or **NR** (non-restrictive) on the line. Then add commas if necessary.*

1. _____ The hotel which was near the waterfall was old and lovely.
_____ The hotel which was near the waterfall was old and lovely.

2. _____ The trip leader who we got to know well was a fascinating person.
_____ The trip leader who we got to know well was a fascinating person.

3. _____ The last day which we spent on the water came too fast.
_____ The last day which we spent on the water came too fast.

C. *Work with a partner. Take turns saying the sentences, paying careful attention to pauses and intonation.*

 READ ABOUT IT!

Recognizing the Author's Purpose in a Brochure

A brochure or pamphlet is a small booklet designed to interest the reader in its subject. Brochures often provide information in pictures, charts or maps, in addition to written information. A brochure may be written for multiple purposes, but generally it is used to persuade the reader to take some action such as visiting a place or buying a product.

The Iditarod! Race Extraordinaire!

You can't compare it to any other competitive event in the world! A race of over 1049 miles of the roughest and most beautiful terrain Mother Nature has to offer. She throws jagged mountain ranges, frozen rivers, dense forests, desolate tundra and miles of windswept coast at the mushers and their dog teams. Add to that temperatures far below zero, winds that can cause a complete loss of visibility, the hazards of overflow, long hours of darkness and treacherous climbs and side hills and you have Iditarod. A race extraordinaire, a race only possible in Alaska.

From Anchorage, in south central Alaska, to Nome on the western Bering Sea Coast, each team of 12 to 20 dogs and their musher cover more than 1049 miles in 11 days to three weeks.

It has been called "The Last Great Race on Earth" and it has won world wide acclaim and interest. German, Spanish, British, Japanese, Australian and American film crews have covered the event. Journalists from outdoor magazines, adventure magazines, national newspapers and wire services flock to Anchorage, Nome, and on the trail between, to record the excitement.

It's not just a dog sled race . . . it's a race in which unique men and women compete. Mushers enter from all walks of life: fishermen, lawyers, doctors, miners, engineers, artists, carpenters, teachers and businessmen. They are from many places: Alaska, the "lower 48," Canada, Great Britain, Australia, Austria, Switzerland, Germany, France, Norway, Italy and Japan. Men and women, each with their own story, each with their own reason for being part of this adventure.

It's a race organized and run by volunteers—over 1,000 volunteers—men, women, and young people from all parts of the world.

On the trail . . .

Every musher has a different tactic. Each one has a special menu for feeding and snacking the dogs. Each one has a different strategy—some run in the daylight, some run at night. Each one has a different training schedule and his own ideas on dog care, dog stamina, and his own personal ability.

Some spend an entire year raising money and getting ready for the race to Nome. Some prepare around a full time job. Hundreds of hours and hundreds of miles of training have to be put in on each team.

There are names which are automatically associated with the race. Dorothy G. Page and Joe Redington Sr., race founders, affectionately known as the ''mother'' and the ''father'' of the Iditarod. Rick Swenson, the only four time winner. Dick Mackey, who beat Swenson by one second in 1978 and achieved the only photo finish in Iditarod's history. Norman Vaughan, the octogenarian adventurer who has completed the race four times and is still competing. Libby Riddles, the first woman to win the Iditarod. Susan Butcher, the only winner of three consecutive races. The list goes on. Each musher, whether in the top ten, or winner of the red lantern (last place) has accomplished a feat few dare attempt. Each has gone the distance, and established a place for his team in the annals of Iditarod lore.

For More Information

Whether you want to run the race, be a volunteer, sponsor a musher, or buy souvenirs, come to Iditarod Headquarters, Mile 2.2 Knik Road, Wasilla, Alaska. It's open five days a week during the winter and every day during the summer months. We look forward to having you involved.

 **EXERCISE 13:** *North to Alaska*

A. *Work with a partner. List at least three purposes of the Iditarod brochure. Does the brochure carry out those purposes in an effective way? Share your ideas with the class.*

B. *What effect does the brochure have on you? Would you like to get more information? find out more about Alaska? go to Alaska and join the race? Or does the brochure make you want to go to a warm place and sit in the sun? Share your ideas.*

 ## SPEAK OUT!

Comparing and Contrasting

In speaking, we often do not state a comparison completely. When a comparison is not completely stated, we must be careful to avoid confusion about the items being compared. Usually the context supplies the needed clues.

> **A:** Do you like mountain climbing?
> **B:** Yes, but I like cave exploring better.

In this case, **. . . better than I like mountain climbing** is clearly understood. Sometimes, however, it is not clear which items are being compared.

> Martin likes dog sled racing better than his wife.

A confused listener might think Martin likes dog sled racing better than he likes his wife, when in fact the speaker means that he likes dog sled racing better than his wife likes dog sled racing! To avoid confusion in cases like this it is better to use both a subject and an auxiliary verb after **than.**

> Martin likes dog sled racing better than his wife does.

EXERCISE 14: *Fire and Ice*

Another dangerous race for adventure lovers is the desert Paris-Dakar race. Participants start out in Paris, France, and finish in Dakar, Senegal. The complicated route involves crossing parts of a desert, where high temperatures, sandstorms, and difficult terrain contribute to the challenge. To win the race, participants use everything from buses to motorcycles to camels. Work with a partner. Compare and contrast the Paris-Dakar race with the Iditarod. Which race would you like to see? participate in?

WRITE ABOUT IT!

Concluding Paragraphs

As you learned in Unit 7, a concluding paragraph summarizes the main ideas developed and brings an essay to an end. It is important to tailor the last paragraph carefully so that those ideas have maximum effect upon the audience. To achieve this, writers restate their strongest ideas in direct, easily followed language that carries a tone of authority and finality. They clearly signal their concluding statements with expressions such as **therefore, finally,** and **in conclusion.**

Writing an Essay Identifying a Problem and Proposing a Solution

One common type of essay describes a problem and then proposes a solution for it. The introductory paragraph of an essay of this kind identifies the problem, while the body paragraphs point out the consequences of leaving the problem unsolved, the importance of a solution, and finally the writer's proposed solution. The concluding paragraph then briefly restates the problem and the writer's solution in an authoritative, convincing way.

EXERCISE 15: *Solving a Problem*

Choose a topic of interest to you from the list and write a multi-paragraph essay outlining the problem and your solution. Show a partner your first draft. Revise your draft and share your essay with the class.

1. the use of animals in competitive sports
2. violent sports
3. too much work, too few vacations
4. your own idea

THINK ABOUT IT!

All of us have opinions about the events, the people, and the things that are part of our lives. We may keep our opinions to ourselves, or we may talk about them with others. The exchange of opinions is an important part of communication. The chart contains some situations in which people might exchange opinions. In which situations are you most likely to bring up your opinions? Fill in the chart.

If you were:	Would you discuss your opinions?	on which subjects?	Would you expect to hear others' opinions? whose?	on which subjects?
meeting a classmate's parents				
meeting a new boss				
at a political rally				
coming out of a movie theater				

TALK IT OVER!

What do you think the cartoonist is trying to say? Discuss your ideas with the class.

PEANUTS reprinted by permission of UFS, Inc.

READ ABOUT IT!

Recognizing Nonstandard English

A. One characteristic that all languages have in common is that there are many spoken varieties of the language. Variations of English may be a result of where the speaker is from, the speaker's age, social class, or level of education. These differences may be in pronunciation, vocabulary, intonation, or structure. For color and authenticity, authors sometimes include nonstandard English in their texts. Have you noticed nonstandard forms in the English you hear or read? What were they? Were you able to understand them? What did the speaker mean? Discuss your experiences with the class.

B. As you read Alice Childress' "The Pocketbook Game," underline examples of nonstandard English you recognize.

The Pocketbook Game
by Alice Childress

Marge . . . Day's work is an education! Well, I mean workin' in different homes you learn much more than if you was steady in one place. . . . I tell you, it really keeps your mind sharp tryin' to watch for what folks will put over on you.

5   What? . . . No, Marge, I do not want to help shell no beans, but I'd be more than glad to stay and have supper with you, and I'll wash the dishes after. Is that all right? . . .

Who put anything over on who? . . . Oh yes! It's like this. . . . I been working for Mrs. E . . . one day a week for several
10 months and I notice that she has some peculiar ways. Well, there was only one thing that really bothered me and that was her pocketbook habit. . . . No, not those little novels. . . . I mean her purse—her handbag.

Marge, she's got a big old pocketbook with two long straps on
15 it . . . and whenever I'd go there, she'd be propped up in a chair with her handbag double wrapped tight around her wrist, and from room to room she'd roam with that purse hugged to her bosom . . . yes, girl! This happens every time! No, there's nobody there but me and her. . . . Marge, I couldn't say nothin'
20 to her! It's her purse, ain't it? She can hold onto it if she wants to! I held my peace for months, tryin' to figure out how I'd make my point. . . . Well, bless Bess! Today was the day! . . . Please, Marge, keep shellin' the beans so we can eat! I know you're listenin', but you listen with your ears, not your hands. . . . Well,
25 anyway, I was almost ready to go home when she steps in the room hangin' onto her bag as usual and says, "Mildred, will you ask the super to come up and fix the kitchen faucet?" "Yes, Mrs. E . . ." I says, "as soon as I leave." "Oh, no," she says, "he may be gone by then. Please go now." "All right," I says, and
30 out the door I went, still wearin' my Hoover apron.

I just went down the hall and stood there a few minutes . . . and then I rushed back to the door and knocked on it as hard and frantic as I could. She flung open the door sayin', "What's the matter? Did you see the super?" . . . "No," I says, gaspin' hard
35 for breath, "I was almost downstairs when I remembered . . . I left my pocketbook!"

With that I dashed in, grabbed my purse and then went down to get the super! Later, when I was leavin' she says real timid-like, "Mildred, I hope that you don't think I distrust you
40 because . . ." I cut her off real quick. . . . "That's all right, Mrs. E . . . , I understand. 'Cause if I paid anybody as little as you pay me, I'd hold my pocketbook too!"

Marge, you fool . . . lookout! . . . You gonna drop the beans on the floor!

EXERCISE 1: *Meaning from Context*

A. *Match the words in column 1 with the meanings in column 2. Write the letter on the line.*

_____ **1.** steady *(line 2)*

_____ **2.** put over on *(lines 4, 8)*

_____ **3.** peculiar *(line 10)*

_____ **4.** hold my peace *(line 21)*

_____ **5.** make my point *(lines 21–22)*

_____ **6.** knock on *(line 32)*

_____ **7.** frantic *(line 33)*

_____ **8.** cut off *(line 40)*

a. keep quiet
b. strange; unusual
c. get an idea across
d. regularly
e. interrupt someone
f. fool, trick
g. take advantage of
h. desperately, urgently
i. hit, struck

B. *At the end of her story, the author uses a number of words associated with **being in a hurry**. How many can you find? Fill in the map with examples from the text and any others you know.*

hurry

DISCUSSION

1. What is the relationship between Mildred and Mrs. E? How do you know?

2. Why do you think the author called her story "The Pocketbook Game"?

📖 **EXERCISE 2:** *Understanding Nonstandard English*

*For each of these examples of nonstandard English from the story, make a **standard** English phrase or sentence with the same meaning.*

1. Well, I mean workin' in different homes you learn much more than if you **was** steady in one place.
2. No, Marge, I do not want to help shell **no** beans, but I'd be more than glad to stay and have supper with you, and I'll wash the dishes after.
3. It's her purse, **ain't** it?
4. "Yes, Mrs. E . . ." I **says**, "as soon as I leave."
5. You **gonna** drop the beans on the floor!

Paraphrasing

As you know, paraphrasing is restating in a different way what someone has said or written. We paraphrase in order to simplify a complicated thought, to emphasize an important point, or to clarify meaning.

📖 **EXERCISE 3:** *In Other Words*

Circle the letter of the best paraphrase.

1. I been working for Mrs. E . . . one day a week for several months and I notice that she has some peculiar ways.
   a. I work for Mrs. E one day a week, and I don't understand the ways she does things.
   b. I've worked for Mrs. E for a while, and I've noticed that she has some unusual habits.
   c. When I was working for Mrs. E, I noticed that she had some unusual habits.

2. . . . from room to room she'd roam with that purse hugged to her bosom . . . .
   a. She held her purse close to her chest in every room of her apartment.
   b. She had walked all around her apartment with her purse on her chest.
   c. She always walked around her apartment holding her purse close to her chest.

📖 🗺 **EXERCISE 4:** *Making Inferences*

A. *Circle **T** for true or **F** for false.*

1. **T F** Marge and Mildred live together.
2. **T F** Mildred thought Mrs. E didn't trust her.
3. **T F** Mildred had spoken to Mrs E about her pocketbook several times before the day of the story.
4. **T F** Marge is interested in Mildred's story.
5. **T F** Mildred thinks Mrs E should pay her more money.

B. *How do you think Mrs. E was planning to finish her last sentence? Share your ideas with the class.*

WORD FOR WORD!

The word **put** is a very common English verb. It is used in a number of two- and three-word verbs. How many can you think of? Make a list.

 EXERCISE 5: *Put It All Together*

Read the conversation and figure out the meaning of the expressions with **put.** *Write the number of the expression on the line next to its meaning.*

SHIRLEY: Hey, Harry! Come here a minute!

HARRY: Just a second—let me finish **(1)** *putting away* these clothes.

SHIRLEY: Oh, **(2)** *put* that *aside* and come and talk to me.

HARRY: OK, OK. What is it?

SHIRLEY: Well, I've **(3)** *put in* a lot of time thinking about this and . . .

HARRY: Uh oh. What?

SHIRLEY: I just wanted to tell you what a great person I think you are to have **(4)** *put up with* me for all these years.

HARRY: You're **(5)** *putting* me *on.*

SHIRLEY: No, I mean it. You never **(6)** *put* me *down* when I have ideas, and you never get mad if I try to **(7)** *put one over on* you.

HARRY: I have a feeling you're **(8)** *putting something over on* me right now.

SHIRLEY: No! I just think that I've **(9)** *put off* telling you how wonderful you are for too long.

HARRY: Thanks. Now why did you ask me to come out here?

SHIRLEY: Well, now that you mention it, I was wondering what you thought of the idea of **(10)** *putting up* a basketball court out here in the backyard. Now Harry—Harry! Come back here!

_____ **a.** joking with
_____ **b.** fooling
_____ **c.** taking to their place
_____ **d.** acted too slowly
_____ **e.** spent
_____ **f.** play a trick on
_____ **g.** ignore temporarily
_____ **h.** think less of
_____ **i.** building
_____ **j.** tolerated

 # SPEAK OUT!

Expressing Understanding and Tolerance

When we express understanding or tolerance, we show that we are willing to listen to another person's point of view. Others are more likely to listen to our ideas if we listen to theirs. In the conversation on page 128, underline the words and expressions the speakers use to indicate they have heard and understood each other's position.

DOUG: You know, I'm having a hard time deciding who to vote for.

MEI: What do you mean?

DOUG: Well, Rosemary Lewis has a lot of positions I agree with, but so does Michael Armstrong. I just can't seem to make up my mind.

MEI: Well, in my opinion, there just aren't enough women in government in this country. So I'm voting for Lewis.

TONY: Wait a minute, Mei. You mean you're voting for her just because she's a woman?

MEI: Well, yes. I agree with some of her ideas, but the important thing to me is that women are under-represented. I just feel that that has to change, and as soon as possible!

DOUG: I'm sure you're right about that, but what about what she stands for? Isn't that important?

TONY: Yes, it is. It's much *more* important, if you ask me. She's always said she was against building a new high school, and as far as I'm concerned that's the number one issue in this campaign.

DOUG: Yes, I see what you mean. We really need the new building.

TONY: Yes, and Armstrong is for it. And I really agree with his ideas on budget reform and public transportation, too. I also feel strongly that we shouldn't vote for or against people just because of their sex, or race, or age. Their ideas are the thing that really matters.

MEI: OK, I see your point. Positions *are* important. But we need people in government to represent both sexes and all races and all ages to serve as role models. Even if their views aren't always the same as mine, they are *there*, and that makes it easier for other women and minorities to get there in the future.

TONY: I see what you're saying. But for me the present, and the new school, are more important.

MEI: Well, I can understand how you would feel that way, but you know, Lewis isn't against schools. Yesterday she said it would be better to fix up the old school and save the money for new books and teachers' salaries.

TONY: Maybe. But I've made up my mind.

MEI: So what about you, Doug? Are you still having trouble making up your mind?

DOUG: Yes, and listening to you two hasn't made it any easier. You're both so convincing!

EXERCISE 6: *Taking Sides*

A. *What is Mei's opinion about the way to choose a candidate? What is Tony's? What are your own views on choosing a candidate for political office? Share your ideas with a partner.*

B. *Take turns giving your opinions and indicating understanding using the topics. Defend your own thinking but acknowledge your tolerance of your partner's different point of view when necessary.*

1. the use of college entrance exams
2. a person's right to government health care
3. the use of credit cards
4. your own idea

G FIGURE IT OUT!

A. *Reported Speech*

In an old Hindu fable, six blind men went to "see" an elephant for the first time. Each one touched a different part of the elephant. When they went home again, their friends asked them "Did you see the elephant?" "Yes!" they replied. But they could not agree when their friends asked "What was it like?"

The first man, who had touched the elephant's side, said "It's like a huge wall!"
The second man, who had touched the elephant's trunk, exclaimed "It's like a snake!"
The third man, who had touched the elephant's tail, thought "It's like a rope!"
The fourth man, who had touched the elephant's tusk, told his friends "It's like a spear!"
The fifth man, who had touched the elephant's leg, said "I'm sure it's like a tree!"
And the sixth man, who had touched the elephant's ear, announced "It feels just like a fan!"

And the six men argued long into the night about an animal none of them had seen.

Their friends asked them if they had seen the elephant, and they replied that they had. But when their friends asked them what it was like, they could not agree. The first man said that it was like a huge wall. The second man exclaimed that it was like a snake. The third man thought that it was like a rope. The fourth man told his friends that it was like a spear. The fifth man was sure that it was like a tree, and the sixth man announced that it felt just like a fan.

EXERCISE 7: *Now I Remember!*

Use your knowledge of reported speech to match the two halves of the sentences. Write the correct letter on the line.

_____ **1.** In reported speech, we usually change
_____ **2.** We generally do not change the verb tense to report
_____ **3.** To report a **yes/no** question we use
_____ **4.** To report an information question we use
_____ **5.** In reported questions the subject is put before
_____ **6.** Some verbs of reporting require

a. theories, beliefs, or general truths.
b. the verb.
c. an indirect object.
d. the verb tense.
e. **if** or **whether.**
f. a question word.

B. *Modals in Reported Speech*

The verbs **should**, **would**, **can**, **could**, **may**, **might**, **must**, and **ought to** follow various patterns.

"I **must** ask you something," he said.	He said that he **had to** ask her something.
"What **would** you **like** to know?" she asked.	She asked him what he **would like** to know.
"It **might** upset you," he said.	He said that it **might** upset her.
"Oh, no, you **can** ask me anything," she said.	She said that he **could** ask her anything.
"I **should have** asked you long ago," he said.	He said that he **should have** asked her long ago.
"You **must have** had a good reason to wait," she said.	She said that he **must have** had a good reason to wait.
"Maybe I **ought to** just say it," he said.	He said that maybe he **ought to** just say it.
"Yes, my dear," she said, please **do**."	She asked him to **do** so.
"Very well," he said. "**May** I borrow your car for the weekend?"	He asked if he **could** borrow her car for the weekend.

EXERCISE 8: *Pay Attention to Me!*

Here are some rules and suggestions you may have heard at some point in your life. Which ones have you been told you should do? had to do? by whom? Write sentences using reported speech.

1. You should brush your teeth three times a day.
2. You must be on time.
3. You should never talk to strangers.
4. You ought to leave a light on in your house when you go out.
5. You may not stay out late.
6. You can't drive alone until you have a driver's license.

C. *Reporting Verbs*

Some verbs used to report speech require paraphrasing the speaker's original words.

"Please come in," she said.	She **invited** me to come in.
"I really think you ought to get professional advice," he said.	He **advised** me to get professional advice.
"Oh, go ahead—you'll enjoy ice-skating," she said.	She **encouraged** me to try ice-skating.

EXERCISE 9: *Reportedly. . . .*

A. *Which verbs in the list follow the same reporting pattern as the sentences in the box? Underline them, and then compare your choices with those of a partner.*

permit	**explain**	**convince**	**direct**
suggest	**warn**	**reply**	**persuade**
remind	**allow**	**expect**	**inform**

B. *Using each of the verbs in the list, make a true sentence about yourself for your partner.*

LISTEN TO THIS!

We talk to many people during the course of a day, and we modify the way we express ourselves depending on the formality of the situation and the status of the people we are talking to. Who do you express your personal opinions to? Do you express your opinions in the same way to everyone? Why or why not?

 EXERCISE 10: *Express Yourself*

A. *Listen to the conversations Monica had with different people. For each conversation, decide who Monica was probably talking to and whether the situation was formal or informal.*

Conversation	Person Talking To	Level of Formality
1	_____	_____
2	_____	_____
3	_____	_____

B. *Compare your answers with those of a partner. How did you arrive at your answers for part* **A?** *What clues helped you decide? Did you and your partner focus on the same kinds of clues?*

 EXERCISE 11: *In My Own Words*

Listen to the conversations again. Work with a partner. Why is Monica so upset? Rephrase what she had to say in your own words.

 SAY IT CLEARLY!

Emphatic Stress

Emphatic stress is a common feature of spoken language. When we want to give special emphasis or importance to a word or phrase, we say that word or phrase louder. We also vary the pitch of the voice, making the voice go higher.

EXERCISE 12: *Whoops!*

A. *Listen to the sentences. Circle the word or phrase receiving emphatic stress. Compare your answers with those of a partner.*

1. You mean Pat actually came out in public and said that?

2. Yes, and on national television!

3. Just wait 'til the boss finds out!

4. Isn't this great? There'll be a huge scandal at the office!

B. *Work with a partner. Say the conversation aloud. Pay special attention to appropriate places for emphatic stress.*

READ ABOUT IT!

Recognizing Style

An author's style is his or her own characteristic manner of expression; it is *how* a writer or speaker says whatever he or she says. We can analyze the style an author uses in a work in terms of the choice of words, the use of figures of speech, the rhythmic patterns, and the sentence patterns. As you read the article by the poet Gwendolyn Brooks, pay attention to her choice of words, the emphasis given to words and ideas, the rhythm, and the sentence patterns.

Culture and Creative Writing
by Gwendolyn Brooks

The most important development in my field in the last 45 years? My definition of my own portion of the field—creative writing—is two-headed. I was born a Black female. By the age of seven this Black female was possessed by a magnificent devotion to language, a
5 fascination with its resources, its potential. Blackness and love of language have been the executives of my life, have nourished and verified my life, have coordinated my portion of the field.

Gwendolyn Brooks with portrait

   I share this field with several categories of writing Blackness. One contingent wholeheartedly subscribes to Blackness. One contingent
10 runs from Blackness and runs to Blackness, bumping into itself, very often, in the middle of the road. One contingent wholeheartedly subscribes to language exploration and experimentation and is more interested in technique than in subject. One contingent believes that extensive testing of English language resources is traitorous to Black
15 Spirit. (This contingent does not quarrel with the continued use of English!—having learned only "jambo" after tackling Swahili back in the late '60s—but urges that it be LEFT ALONE, left PLAIN: "don't worry about cliches—*they* say what you MEAN; *forget* varnish and flowers and cinnamon.")

20   I cannot say that, in 45 years there has been a definite, forward, delightfully visible, importantly thick line of development in quality, stretch and strength of Black creativity in the field of writing. There has been retreat, bright advance, retreat, bounce-backability. (True of Hispanic and Caucasian creative writing as well. The times have jounced
25 *and* curtailed us all.) But it may be proper to claim, as an Important Development, that there has been a steady growth in *numbers* of Black authors. Many, many talented Blacks of all ages have been writing *seriously* a-down the last 45 years, are writing seriously *now.*

   I am especially excited and encouraged by the talent I see among our
30 children. What are our little children doing? *Yes,* they *are* writing poetry. Poetry is still in the world, and children are colliding with some of it. They reach, touch lovely words and strong words with excitement and timid respect. They work hard to merit ownership. Looking at poetry and saluting it, they realize that in the world there is beauty. That there
35 is horror they know and have always known. New bombs are crafted

most carefully. Hatreds are here, and multiply. Modern ice and iron marry, and offer presently a frightening progeny. But children know also that there are flowers. They are not ashamed to speak to daisies and dandelions. Children of course commit platitudes a-plenty. Often our
40 young poets address their readers and, more sorrowfully, them*selves*, in a cliche-ridden manner that they assume is "right for poetry." But they are capable, also, of exaltation and thought and emotion and expression that do them honor. Their nature is not frugal, it is expansive and lifting. It reacts. It reacts to clouds, sunshine. It reacts to dryness, waste,
45 oppression. Some of these young people . . . have found that poetry is a friend to whom you can say too much. Some of them have found that it is possible, *sometimes,* to reconcile onions and roses.

EXERCISE 13: *It's My Style*

A. *What elements contribute to the style Gwendolyn Brooks uses in her article? What words or phrases caught your eye? How did Brooks use language, emphasis, rhythm, and sentence patterns? Find an example of each in the article and write them on the lines.*

1. choice of words _____

2. figures of speech _____

3. rhythmic patterns _____

4. sentence patterns _____

B. *Did you find the author's style easy to follow? What do you think the author's purpose was? Does her style support her purpose? How? Discuss your answers with the class.*

 # SPEAK OUT!

Emphasizing Strong Convictions

Just as important as the indication of our respect for another person's point of view is the affirmation of our own strong feelings. When we tactfully indicate our very strong opinions on something, we use certain words and expressions that communicate the depth of our feelings without offending the other person. We use expressions such as **I really feel very strongly about this, I cannot modify my opinion on this matter,** and **This means a great deal to me.** These expressions let people know that there is no possibility that you will change your beliefs. What other expressions can you think of that tactfully emphasize the strength of your opinions?

EXERCISE 14: *In My Opinion*

A. *Do you agree with what Brooks has to say about cultural influence and creative writing? Do you agree with her feelings about language, writing, and poetry? Discuss with a partner.*

B. *Work with a partner. Take turns expressing your opinions about the topics in the list. Use the language for indicating understanding of another person's opinion and the language for emphasizing the strength of your own convictions when appropriate.*

1. People around the world should speak one common language, even if it has to be an artificial language.
2. Schools should not use examinations for evaluation.
3. Military service should be voluntary.
4. Students should study science and math, not literature and art.
5. Commercials should not be allowed on television.
6. your own idea

 WRITE ABOUT IT!

Developing an Essay Supporting or Refuting a Position

Organization is especially important when a writer develops an essay to support (to be *for*) or to refute (to be *against*) a position. In a well-organized essay, the reader is more likely to follow the writer's arguments, and as a result, be more receptive to his or her ideas. Effective writers normally use one of two ways to structure this type of essay. Look at the models.

Model 1

Introductory Paragraph: **statement of position**
TV stations should donate time to minorities to express their views on the issues of the day.

Body: **reasons to support this view; the consequences of not supporting this view**

Concluding Paragraph: **restatement of position; restatement of the strongest argument in favor of or against position**

Model 2

Introductory Paragraph: **exposition of problems**
Minorities do not have an impartial, cost-effective way to make their views known to the public.

Body: **the implications of the problems; supporting reasons for the statement of position**

Concluding Paragraph: **strong summing up of the statement of position**

 EXERCISE 15: *Put It in Writing*

Develop one of the topics from the list in Exercise 14. Use any of the prewriting steps you have learned to organize your ideas. Write a multi-paragraph essay developing your position in support of or against the issue you have chosen. When you have finished, show your work to a partner to discuss content, clarity, and organization. Then write your final draft.

THINK ABOUT IT!

A. People have different feelings about water. On a sheet of paper, make a word map about your associations with water.

B. Bill and Rebecca had very different experiences with water. Read their stories.

Bill

I've been afraid of water for as long as I can remember. When I was very little, I fell into a swimming pool and nearly drowned. I remember hearing a strange throbbing sound as I went under water. It was terrifying. The next thing I knew, I was on the side of the pool, and everyone was looking at me. I guess that I never got over it, because ever since then I've stayed away from water. I don't even like to fly over water in a plane. In high school, it was a real problem, because we had to pass a swimming test in order to graduate. Luckily, the teacher gave me a lot of extra help, and I managed to pass.

Rebecca

I remember jumping in the waves at the beach and loving it. My mother and I stayed at the seashore all summer, and my father came from the city on weekends to join us. We spent the whole day at the beach. As soon as I got there, I got in the water and stayed in until lunch time. The splashing water felt so cool and refreshing. After lunch, I'd take a nap under our umbrella. Now I swim twice a week. When I'm in the water, I feel free, relaxed, and refreshed. It's like moving through silk.

How were Bill's and Rebecca's feelings about water formed? How were your feelings formed? Tell a partner a story about your experiences with water.

TALK IT OVER!

A. Where are the different places people can swim? What kinds of activities can we do in or near water? Work with a partner and make lists.

B. Over seven thousand people drown each year in the U.S. What are the causes? How much do you know about water safety? Draw up a list of water safety tips. Compare your list with your partner's.

READ ABOUT IT!

Clarifying Our Purpose in Reading and Choosing an Appropriate Reading Strategy

When we pick up a newspaper or magazine we may be looking for certain topics—international news, local news, sports news, or business news. We may be interested in reading about celebrities, politics, or sports. Sometimes we have a very specific goal, such as finding out movie times, the weather report, an exchange rate, or grocery prices. Sometimes another part of the newspaper or magazine catches our attention, and we change goals as we read. Look briefly at the article "The History of Olympic Swimming." Write two questions you want answered about the topic on the lines.

1. _____

2. _____

Think about the reading strategies you have learned in this book. Which strategy or strategies would you use to find out the answers to your questions? Compare your ideas with those of a partner.

Using Prior Knowledge

As you know, it is much easier to read if we reflect on what we already know about the topic before we read. Do you think the statements are true or false? Write **T** for true, **F** for false, or **DK** for don't know on the line.

_____ **1.** The ancient Olympics started in Rome.
_____ **2.** Athletes in the ancient Olympics competed for gold medals.
_____ **3.** In the ancient games there were only foot races.
_____ **4.** Wars stopped so that people could compete in the ancient games.
_____ **5.** The modern Olympics began about one hundred years ago.
_____ **6.** Swimming has always been part of the modern games.
_____ **7.** Olympic swimming competitions have been held in rivers and lakes.
_____ **8.** The first Olympic swimming pools were smaller than today's.

Mark the facts you want to check when you read the article.

Scanning an Article on History

When we read about **history,** we often want to know **when** and **where** events happened. Scan the article and underline any dates and circle any places.

Duke Kahanamoku, Olympic Gold Medal winner for swimming events 1912 and 1920

The History of Olympic Swimming
by Jerdine Nolen-Harold

The history of the Olympic Games dates back to ancient Athens of 776 B.C., when there was a great foot race of about two hundred yards in the valley of Olympia, in western Greece. The
5 winner was crowned with an olive branch wreath, which, to the ancient Greeks, was a symbol of honor and glory. Fame and immortality followed, as poems and legends told of the winners' accomplishments. These early
10 trials of track and field were open only to men—women were forbidden even as spectators. For centuries, the original Olympic Games were considered so important that even wars were stopped so the games could take place. However, as the glory of Greece faded, so did 15 the games. The games continued under the Roman Empire, but athletes competed mainly for money. Finally, the games were halted by one of the Roman emperors. It would take 1500 years and the vision of one man, Pierre de 20 Coubertin of France, to rekindle the Olympic spirit. After much work, Coubertin saw his dream become reality when the first modern Olympics began on April 6, 1896.

---

25 Over 280 athletes from 13 countries participated in the first modern
Olympics, which, like the ancient games, focused mainly on track and
field events. In fact, not until relatively recently has swimming been
given the same status as track and field. In the 1896 games there were
four men's swimming events, and eleven track and field events. Today
30 the competitive swimming events for both men and women total thirty
and track and field events number around forty-one.

   In the earliest modern games swimmers had enormous obstacles to
overcome. Since swimming pools were not introduced until later,
facilities consisted of the nearest natural body of water, with no clear-
35 cut boundaries, markers, or adequate views for spectators. Swimmers
often did not know what kinds of conditions they would have to face
until they arrived at the site of the games. In the swimming competition
of the Athens games of 1896, which took place in the sea, dried gourds
and flags were used to mark boundaries and finish lines. The water
40 temperature was so low that the U.S. 100-meter swimmer is reported
to have jumped in, screamed, "I'm freezing," and climbed right back out!

   In the next Olympiad, in Paris (1900), two new events were added—
the backstroke and the underwater competition. The swimming events
took place in the Seine, where competitors had to complete a sort of
45 obstacle race sometimes called hurdle swimming in which they had to
swim through barrels over a distance of about fifty meters. This was
the only time the event was ever held. The year 1900 also marked the
first year that women were allowed to compete in the Olympics,
though not in swimming. Women would not be allowed to compete in
50 Olympic swimming until the 1904 games in St. Louis, Missouri.

Johnny Weismuller

   Olympic swimming events continued to be held in lakes, rivers, and
seas until the 1908 games in London, which took place in a pool one
hundred meters long. Competitors could then swim in safer, calmer
waters than before. Facilities for spectators were much improved, too.
55 In fact, attendance at the swimming events in London on one day topped
60,000. Subsequent Olympics took place in pools of this length until the
standard fifty-meter pool was established in the Paris Olympics of 1924.

   Other changes were made over time. By 1956, new strokes had been
added to the official repertoire, including the freestyle. Technical
60 advancements in measuring systems made it possible to record the
swimmers' times with great precision. Swimmers can now be timed as
precisely as 1/1000 of a second!

   As training methods improved and the number of swimming events
grew, amazing records continued to be set. In the Paris Olympics of
65 1924, Johnny Weismuller became the first man to swim one hundred
meters in less than one minute. He collected a total of five gold
medals. Later, because of his fame as a swimmer, he was asked to
play Tarzan in the movies. Even more amazing was the swimming
competition of 1972, which will be remembered for the supreme
70 performance of one individual, Mark Spitz. He won the most gold
medals for swimming at a single Olympics, setting a world record with
each of his seven victories over a period of seven days. Spitz also tried
an acting career, but did not have the same success as Weismuller. The
greatest women Olympic swimmers include Kristin Otto of the former
75 East Germany, who won the most gold medals, six, in the Seoul games
of 1988, and Dawn Frasier of the U.S., who won the most medals, four
gold and four silver, in three different Olympics.

Kristin Otto

The growth of swimming as an Olympic event has paralleled the growth of the modern Olympics, from its small beginnings in 1896 to
80 the huge games of today, with thousands of participants from over 160 countries and hundreds of millions of viewers on television.

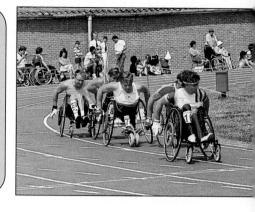

DISCUSSION

1. Are there any poems, stories, or songs about the modern Olympics? How are winners' accomplishments celebrated today?

2. Should there be an international fund to make sure that athletes have an equal opportunity to train before the games?

3. What do you know about the Special Olympics? How are they different from the Olympics?

4. Do the games really promote world peace?

EXERCISE 1: *Meaning from Context*

Match the word in columns 1 and 2 with its meaning in column 3. Write the letter on the line.

_____ **1.** spectator *(line 11)*   _____ **4.** status *(line 28)*
_____ **2.** halt *(line 18)*   _____ **5.** obstacles *(line 32)*
_____ **3.** rekindle *(line 21)*   _____ **6.** site *(line 37)*

a. start
b. place, location
c. things in your way
d. get people interested again
e. person who watches
f. position in society
g. stop

EXERCISE 2: *Comprehension Check*

A. *Did the article answer the questions you wrote on page 136? Check your answers to the true/false activity. How many of your answers were correct?*

B. *Answer the questions on a sheet of paper.*

1. How are the modern Olympics different from the ancient Olympics?
2. How are today's Olympics different from the first modern Olympics?
3. Were there swimming events in the first modern Olympics?

EXERCISE 3: *Reading Strategy Review*

The reading strategy we use depends on our purpose for reading. Imagine that you just bought a newspaper and have the purposes in column 1 in mind. Match the purpose with the strategy in column 2. Write the letter on the line.

_____ **1.** find out the time a play begins
_____ **2.** decide whether the newspaper's articles on a certain topic are biased
_____ **3.** get information on current events in Europe for a report in school
_____ **4.** find out what the weather will be in a city you're flying to this afternoon
_____ **5.** get a general idea about the most important events that are happening around the world

a. skim
b. scan
c. distinguish fact and opinion
d. summarize
e. understand a graph
f. use maps and charts

Making Inferences

The article gives *some* information on the history of Olympic swimming, but we can build on this information by making inferences. For example, when we read that wars were stopped for the Games, we can infer that the Games were probably considered more important than the war.

 EXERCISE 4: *Reading Between the Lines*

Complete the chart, using information from the article and by making inferences. Discuss your answers with a partner.

	Ancient Games	Modern Games
Aims	1.	1.
Events	2.	2.
Participants	3.	3.
Spectators	4.	4.
Prizes	5.	5.

 WORD FOR WORD!

Gabriela Sabatini

Specialized Vocabulary

When we take part in a sport, we learn the specialized vocabulary that goes with it. For example, probably only a skier would know the difference between **powder, wet,** and **corn snow.** What do you think the terms mean? Why would a skier need specialized terms about snow? (For the answers, check page 146.)

EXERCISE 5: *The Vocabulary of Sports*

Use words from the list to complete the chart. Some words can be used more than once.

ball	**kick**	**match**	**marathon**	**sprint**	**whites**
basket	**game**	**swim**	**brake**	**race**	**runner**
bike	**throw**	**meet**	**float**	**swimmer**	**track meet**
dash	**helmet**	**pedal**	**serve**	**jog**	**swimsuit**
dribble	**racket**	**player**	**shoes**	**track suit**	**cyclist**

Sport	Player	Equipment and Clothes	Event	Actions
swimming	**swimmer**			**swim, kick**
running				**jog**
basketball				
bicycling				
tennis				

Sports Idioms

Many sports expressions have become so common that they have become idioms that apply to all situations, not just sports.

 EXERCISE 6: *It's Your Serve*

*Use the context to figure out the meaning of the words in **dark type.** Write the letter on the line.*

_____ **1.** Hey, did you hear? Tim won $20 million in the lottery! He's **swimming in** money!

_____ **2.** Next, Barbara is going to speak to us about the project schedule. Barbara, **it's your serve.**

_____ **3.** Gloria, I can't finish all my work before I leave on vacation. I'm afraid I'm going to have **to pass the ball** to you. Can you help me?

_____ **4.** Susan is in trouble. She has two tests tomorrow and she hasn't even studied. She's **in deep water.**

_____ **5.** Dolores is really **on the ball.** She is the most efficient secretary we've ever had—everything gets done!

a. It's your turn.
b. someone who works quickly and well
c. to give to someone else to continue
d. in trouble
e. has a lot of

SPEAK OUT!

Talking About Advantages and Disadvantages

When we talk of advantages and disadvantages we often use the language of comparison and contrast (Units 3, 10), conditionals (Unit 6), and the language of opinions and preferences (Units 4, 7, 11).

> Swimming is a gentle exercise, whereas jogging can put stress on your knees and ankles.
> This book says that if I jog every day, I'll lose more weight than if I swim every day.
> In my opinion, it's better to exercise outdoors than in a health club.

Which sentences show the language of comparison and contrast? conditionals? opinions and preferences?

EDDIE: Hi, Shelley. You look excited. What's up?

SHELLEY: I've just had a call from the beach office. They want to interview me for a job as a lifeguard.

EDDIE: Congratulations! You deserve it. You're the best swimmer I know!

SHELLEY: Thanks. But there's also a job opening at the pool. If I work there, it'll be less stressful. At the pool you almost never see a swimmer in trouble, whereas at the beach, there's always the chance of someone swimming too far from shore and getting in trouble.

EDDIE: But don't you think the beach job would be more fun?

SHELLEY: Maybe, but the job at the pool has longer hours and pays better. The beach closes at five o'clock, but the pool stays open until ten during the week and midnight on weekends.

EDDIE: The good thing about being a lifeguard at the beach is that you can talk to all your friends, like me, anytime, because that's where we'll be—the beach is free!

SHELLEY: Hey! That's where you're wrong! As a lifeguard, I'm not allowed to chat—in either place. I can *wave* to my friends, but not talk to them.

EDDIE: Too bad. Well, I still prefer the beach. The pool is much more crowded and noisy from all the little children there.

SHELLEY: Yes, sometimes it's so crowded that the guards have to make people get out of the pool. And the noise *is* awful sometimes. But being a lifeguard is very satisfying. When I help someone in trouble, it's the most incredible feeling in the world!

EXERCISE 7: *Pros and Cons*

A. *List the advantages and disadvantages of each job Shelley is considering.*

Pool		Beach	
Advantages	Disadvantages	Advantages	Disadvantages

B. *Work with a partner. What should Shelley do? Which job would you accept? Compare your lists of pros and cons.*

EXERCISE 8: *On the Other Hand*

A. *Work with a partner. Make a list of the advantages and disadvantages of the topics.*

as transportation to work: walking, driving, riding the bus, bicycling, taking a taxi

as a way to exercise: aerobics, yoga, football, skating, hiking

B. *Compare your list with that of another pair of students. As a group, discuss the advantages and disadvantages of the topics and make one list in which you rank the advantages and disadvantages of each topic in order of importance.*

 FIGURE IT OUT!

A. *Cause and Effect*

When we state the consequences of actions, we can use several structures.

> The water was dirty. **Consequently,** the swimmers complained.
> The pool was dirty. **Therefore,** the swim meet had to be
>   moved.
> The best swimmer was sick, **so** the team lost.

 EXERCISE 9: *So Then What Happened?*

Describe the effects of the events. Write sentences on a sheet of paper.

1. In 1896, Olympic swimming events took place in a harbor.
2. A one-hundred meter pool was used in 1904.
3. Clocks for timing swimmers are now very precise.
4. The Olympics are now televised worldwide.

B. *Comparatives and Superlatives*

As you know, we use **-er/-est, more, most, fewer, fewest, less,** and **least** to form comparative and superlative forms of adjectives, adverbs, and nouns. Go back to the article on Olympic swimming. Circle all of the examples of comparative and superlative structures.

> Olympic Facts
> - The countries that participate **most consistently** in the summer games are Austria, France, Greece, Britain, and Switzerland, which have never missed the games.
> - Countries participate **less regularly** in the winter games. Only Britain has never been absent. (This is because the winter games are **newer,** and winter sports are considered **less important** than summer sports.)
> - The **largest** crowd at any Olympic event was 150,000 at the ski jumping at the 1952 Olympics in Norway.
> - The **most popular** event is usually the opening ceremony.
> - The person with **the most** gold medals is Clarence Ewry of the U.S., with ten.
> - The woman with **the highest** number of medals is Vera Caslavska of Czechoslovakia, with seven.
> - The person with **the most** gold medals for swimming events in a single Olympics is Mark Spitz of the U.S., who swam **the fastest** in seven events.
>
> There are also records for the countries that have won **the fewest medals,** for the events that are **the least popular,** and for countries that spend **the least** money on their teams. But no one discusses these records much, because people are **more interested** in talking about winners!

EXERCISE 10: *I Know That!*

Circle the answer or answers.

1. To compare count nouns, we use:

    -er/-est   **more/most**   **fewer/fewest**   **less/least**

2. To compare mass nouns, we use

    -er/-est   **more/most**   **fewer/fewest**   **less/least**

3. To compare adverbs, we use

    -er/-est   **more/most**   **fewer/fewest**   **less/least**

EXERCISE 11: *The Games Yesterday and Today*

Use the information in the article on pages 136 and 137 to write ten sentences on a sheet of paper comparing the early Olympics with those of today.

C. *Expressing the Strength of Our Ideas*

We can use intensifiers to convey the strength of our ideas.

> Going to the Olympics was **really** exciting!
> Winning an Olympic medal was **awfully** exciting!

Is **awfully** positive or negative in this context? How can you tell?

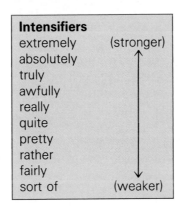

Intensifiers

extremely	(stronger)
absolutely	
truly	
awfully	
really	
quite	
pretty	
rather	
fairly	
sort of	(weaker)

EXERCISE 12: *Memorable Moments*

*Complete each sentence with an appropriate intensifier, or an adjective, an adverb, or a noun with **-er/-est, more/most, less/least,** or **fewer/fewest**. Write your answers on a sheet of paper.*

Well, Ladies and Gentlemen, the Olympics are about to begin. This is a **(1)** _____ impressive occasion. Thousands of the world's **(2)** _____ athletes are here for the **(3)** _____ sport event of the year. There are even **(4)** _____ countries participating than four years ago. Soon they'll be marching into the stadium. Then we'll watch the **(5)** _____ dramatic moment of the opening—the lighting of the Olympic flame!

    This year, many countries have increased the number of athletes on their teams, so there is **(6)** _____ competition than four years ago. As in all the past Olympics, we can expect to see some **(7)** _____ amazing feats of athletic ability! Look, here come the athletes!

LISTEN TO THIS!

When we talk to people who are not familiar with our special interests, we explain the specialized vocabulary and concepts they may not know. Work with a partner. Look at the picture of the scuba diver and describe how the diver uses the equipment.

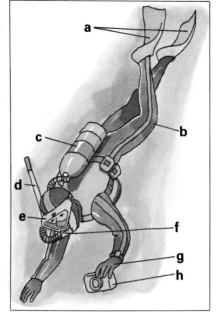

 EXERCISE 13: *Rapture of the Deep*

A. *What equipment does a scuba diver use? Listen to the conversation and underline the equipment you hear.*

socks	goggles	camera
gloves	snorkel	wet suit
boat	mouthpiece	spear
air tanks	regulator	weights
mask	flashlight	knife
rocks	cap	fins

B. *Listen again and label the picture. Write the word on the line.*

a. _____

b. _____

c. _____

 SAY IT CLEARLY!

d. _____

Thought Groups

e. _____

When we say a series of words, phrases (including groups of numbers), or clauses in a sentence, we pause, and our intonation changes at the end of each item in the series. Listen to the examples. The phrases are marked with **|**. Mark rising intonation with ↑ and falling intonation with ↓.

f. _____

g. _____

h. _____

> My phone number is 708 | 555 | 1212.
> And here's my student I.D. number | my driver's license number | and my parking sticker number.

EXERCISE 14: *Next, Please!*

A. *Listen and mark the groups in column 2 with* **|**.

A: Your address?

B: It's 1403 West 5th Street Santa Ana, California 93121.

A: Your phone number?

B: It's 5554321.

A: What classes are you taking?

B: English, French, and History.

B. *Listen again and mark the intonation of the groups in column 2. Use ↑ for rising intonation and ↓ for falling intonation.*

C. *Work with a partner. Take turns asking each other the questions in column 1. Answer about yourself. Use correct intonation.*

READ ABOUT IT!

Figuring Out the Intended Audience

As you know, writers usually aim their articles at a certain audience. This article appeared in a magazine. What type of audience do you think the writer had in mind?

Walking—one of the kindest, gentlest forms of working out—can tone you up and trim you down. And it burns about as many calories as jogging or aerobics.

Whether you're on the street window shopping, in a park smelling the flowers, or on an electronic treadmill, walking briskly is one of the most effective, convenient, and safe ways to get into shape. Before you say walking is for wimps, consider these facts.

Walking a mile in 12 minutes burns about 86 calories for a 120-pound person, about the same number as jogging the same distance.

Walking tightens and tones legs and thighs. And, by walking on an incline—either going up hill or using a computerized treadmill—you can also trim down your stomach, hips, shoulders, and arms.

Walking is virtually injury-free. And it is beneficial for people who do not work out or participate in sports regularly, says Ron Jacobs, trainer and owner of The Walking Center in Beverly Hills, California.

Walking regularly may reduce your risk of dying from heart disease and cancer, according to a recent study published in the *Journal of the American Medical Association*.

EXERCISE 15: *A Sporting Chance*

A. *Work with a partner. What kind of exercise would you recommend for these people?*

a teenage girl   a grandfather   a taxi driver   an executive

B. *Imagine that you and your partner have to write an article to convince people to take up one of the sports you recommended in* **A.** *How would you shape the article to the intended audience? What kinds of information and details would you use to interest that audience?*

SPEAK OUT!

Expressing Fear and Dismay

When we learn something new, such as a new sport, it's natural to experience fear and dismay. Read the expressions. What other expressions can we use to express fear and dismay?

Think of a time when you learned to do something new. Did you have an instructor? How did you feel? What did you think or say?

> I'm scared.
> I don't think I can do this.
> Can you give me a hand?
> I'll never make it.

Encouraging and Congratulating

When we learn new things, our teachers encourage us to keep on trying as we learn, and congratulate us when we succeed.

Read the conversation. How do the people express fear and dismay? offer encouragement and congratulations?

Hang in there.	Well done!
Keep at it.	You did it!
Try again.	That's great!
You can do it.	Congratulations!

> A: OK, are you ready to try again?
> B: I guess. I'm afraid I'll fall again.
> A: Never mind. I'll help you. Just put your foot on the top pedal.
> B: Like this?
> A: Way to go! Now push. Keep your balance. Keep going. Push with your other foot. That's good. . . .
> B: Oh, I'm going to fall!!
> A: No, you're not. Try again. You'll get it.

 EXERCISE 16: *Way to Go!*

Work with a partner. Teach your partner how to do an exercise, such as a sit-up or a toe touch, or an activity from a sport you know well. Offer encouragement and congratulations.

 WRITE ABOUT IT!

Writing to Report Opinions and Draw Conclusions

Often as writers we are called upon to examine differing opinions about a topic and then draw a conclusion about which opinion is better. The model shows one common way to organize an essay of this type.

Introductory Paragraph:	**Statement of two opinions** Many people are of the opinion that professionals should be permitted to participate in the Olympics. Others, however, feel that the Olympics should remain an event for amateurs.
Body:	**Explanation of one opinion** **Explanation of second opinion** **Comparison of two opinions**
Concluding Paragraph:	**Conclusion** about which opinion is better **Restatement** of strongest reason why

 EXERCISE 17: *What's Your Conclusion?*

Write a multi-paragraph essay reporting two opposing opinions on a topic of your choice. Examine each opinion carefully, and then draw your own conclusion as to which opinion is better. Follow the steps of the writing process.

Answer to Word for Word (page 139)

Wet snow has heavy, large flakes with a lot of moisture. Powder snow is dry snow with small, light flakes. Corn snow is pellets the size of corn kernels, formed by successive melting and freezing at high altitudes. Skiers have so many terms because the type of snow affects skiing conditions. Powder snow usually offers the best skiing conditions.

UNIT 12 IN THE SWIM!

IRREGULAR VERBS

Base Form	Simple Past	Past Participle	Base Form	Simple Past	Past Participle
be, am, is, are	was, were	been	lie	lay	lain
become	became	become	let	let	let
begin	began	begun	lose	lost	lost
blow	blew	blown	make	made	made
break	broke	broken	mean	meant	meant
bring	brought	brought	meet	met	met
build	built	built	pay	paid	paid
buy	bought	bought	put	put	put
catch	caught	caught	quit	quit	quit
choose	chose	chosen	read	read	read
come	came	come	ride	rode	ridden
cost	cost	cost	run	ran	run
cut	cut	cut	say	said	said
dig	dug	dug	see	saw	seen
do	did	done	sell	sold	sold
draw	drew	drawn	send	sent	sent
drink	drank	drunk	set	set	set
drive	drove	driven	sing	sang	sung
eat	ate	eaten	sit	sat	sat
fall	fell	fallen	sleep	slept	slept
feel	felt	felt	speak	spoke	spoken
find	found	found	speed	sped	sped
fight	fought	fought	spend	spent	spent
fit	fit	fit	split	split	split
fly	flew	flown	stand	stood	stood
forget	forgot	forgotten	steal	stole	stolen
get	got	gotten	stick	stuck	stuck
give	gave	given	strike	struck	struck
go	went	gone	swim	swam	swum
grow up	grew up	grown up	take	took	taken
have, has	had	had	tell	told	told
hear	heard	heard	think	thought	thought
hide	hid	hidden	throw	threw	thrown
hit	hit	hit	understand	understood	understood
hold	held	held	wake	woke	woken
hurt	hurt	hurt	wear	wore	worn
keep	kept	kept	win	won	won
know	knew	known	write	wrote	written
leave	left	left			

THE INTERNATIONAL PHONETIC ALPHABET

IPA SYMBOLS

CONSONANTS
/b/   **b**a**b**y, clu**b**
/d/   **d**own, to**d**ay, sa**d**
/f/   **f**un, pre**f**er, lau**gh**
/g/   **g**ood, be**g**in, do**g**
/h/   **h**ome, be**h**ind
/k/   **k**ey, cho**c**olate, bla**ck**
/l/   **l**ate, po**l**ice, mai**l**
/m/   **m**ay, wo**m**an, swi**m**
/n/   **n**o, opi**n**io**n**
/ŋ/   a**ng**ry, lo**ng**
/p/   **p**a**p**er, ma**p**
/r/   **r**ain, pa**r**ent, doo**r**
/s/   **s**alt, medi**c**ine, bu**s**
/š/   **s**ugar, spe**ci**al, fi**sh**
/t/   **t**ea, ma**t**erial, da**t**e
/θ/   **th**ing, heal**th**y, ba**th**
/ð/   **th**is, mo**th**er, ba**th**e
/v/   **v**ery, tra**v**el, o**f**
/w/   **w**ay, any**o**ne
/y/   **y**es, on**i**on
/z/   **z**oo, cou**s**in, alway**s**
/ž/   mea**s**ure, gara**g**e
/č/   **ch**eck, pic**t**ure, wa**tch**
/ǰ/   **j**ob, re**f**ri**g**erator, oran**g**e

VOWELS
/ɑ/   **o**n, h**o**t, f**a**ther
/æ/   **a**nd, c**a**sh
/ɛ/   **e**gg, s**ay**s, l**ea**ther
/ɪ/   **i**n, b**i**g
/ɔ/   **o**ff, d**au**ghter, dr**aw**
/e/   **A**pril, tr**ai**n, s**ay**
/i/   **e**ven, sp**ea**k, tr**ee**
/o/   **o**pen, cl**o**se, sh**ow**
/u/   b**oo**t, d**o**, thr**ough**
/ʌ/   **o**f, y**ou**ng, s**u**n
/ʊ/   p**u**t, c**oo**k, w**ou**ld
/ə/   **a**bout, penc**i**l, lem**o**n
/ɚ/   moth**er**, Satu**r**day, doct**or**
/ɜ/   **ear**th, b**ur**n, h**er**

Diphthongs
/ɑɪ/   **i**ce, st**y**le, l**ie**
/ɑʊ/   **ou**t, d**ow**n, h**ow**
/ɔɪ/   **oi**l, n**oi**se, b**oy**

THE ENGLISH ALPHABET

Here is the pronunciation of the letters of the English alphabet, written in International Phonetic Alphabet symbols.

a   /e/
b   /bi/
c   /si/
d   /di/
e   /i/
f   /ɛf/
g   /ǰi/
h   /eč/
i   /ɑɪ/
j   /ǰe/
k   /ke/
l   /ɛl/
m   /ɛm/
n   /ɛn/
o   /o/
p   /pi/
q   /kyu/
r   /ɑr/
s   /ɛs/
t   /ti/
u   /yu/
v   /vi/
w   /ˈdʌbəlˌyu/
x   /ɛks/
y   /wɑɪ/
z   /zi/

GETTING STARTED

Nouns
concerns
interpretation
optimist
passion
pessimist
soul
tips

Verb
to gain

Adjectives
secret
specific

UNIT 1

Science
behavior
hypothesis
laboratory
subjective

Other Nouns
anecdote
bar graph
intent
parrot
reward
signal
whale

Verbs
to correlate
to endanger
to grasp
to mimic
to perceive
to process

Adjectives
accurate
capable

Expressions
birdbrain
black sheep
bookworm
catnip
crocodile tears
dog-tired
fishy
goose bumps
rat race
road hog
wild-goose chase

UNIT 2

Literature
autobiography
biography
data
research
subject (of a
    biography)

Other Nouns
background
    (economic)
credibility
failure
objective
pattern
portion
poverty
prejudice
scholarship

Verbs
to be somebody
to cover
to drop out
to eat up
to endure
to exert
to flunk
to get (one's) way
to suffer
to throw (one's
    self) into

Adjectives
available
eccentric
tender
tough

Expression
true grit

UNIT 3

Film
critic
director
festival
masterpiece
producer
screenwriter
scriptwriter
thriller

Other Nouns
attitude
corruption
impact
minority
novelist
rebellion
sponsor
tolerance

Verbs
to adapt
to dare
to derive
to incorporate
to interpret
to stimulate

Adjectives
controversial
definitive
extensive
ironic
neutral
pessimistic
unflattering
unique

UNIT 4

Nouns
absence
brevity
category
disadvantage
fuss
insight
instruction
leavetaking
occasion
questionnaire
suburbs
tone

Verbs
to abandon
to deny
to focus
to go over
to interact
to keep in
to keep up
to reject
to stick to
to tune in

Adjectives
ambiguous
appropriate
firm
literal
reluctant
tentative

UNIT 5

Fireworks
bang
casualty
display
explosive
firecracker
firework
pyrotechnician
tradition

Other Nouns
ban
descendant
gist
headline
inference
origin
repose

Verbs
to justify
to recycle
to relate
to restrict
to transform
to turn (become)

Adjectives
costly
isolated
lethal
odd
old-fashioned
remarkable
renowned
risky
unpredictable
varied

UNIT 6

Food and Cooking
edibles
lobster
melon
nutrition
oven
potluck dinner
seafood
shrimp
turkey
yogurt

Other Nouns
face mask
factors

Verbs
to clear up
to convey
to cover up
to dig in
to motivate
to speculate
to spoil
to warm

Adjectives
allergic
astringent
bent over
burned
oily
plentiful
polite
refreshing
roasted
scrumptious
superior
undesirable

UNIT 7

Music
disco
gospel
heavy metal
rap
reggae

Other Nouns
atmosphere
costumes
debate
destiny
euphemism
frenzy
image
lighting
reflection
taste

Verbs
to appeal
to coin
to evolve
to skip

Adjectives
additional
consecutive
dissent
essential
indelible
lucrative
melancholy
promising
tragic

UNIT 8

Personality
extrovert
introvert
psychologist
realist
type (kind)

Other Nouns
assertion
assessment
consensus
merit

Verbs
to generalize
to get over
to keep track of
to label
to look down on
to put up with
to reassure
to run into
to stay away from
to think over

Adjectives
abrupt
clumsy
complicated
humiliating
predictable
sentimental
subsequent
well-adjusted

Adverb
arbitrarily

UNIT 9

Maps and Geography
archipelago
bay
canal
canyon
cartographer
channel
cliff
coast
delta

geographer
harbor
mapmaker
peninsula
shoreline
swamp
valley
zone

Other Nouns
bias
statistics

Verbs
to concede
to exaggerate
to feature
to reveal
to sketch
to visualize

Adjectives
distinctive
misleading
populated
prominent

Adverb
densely

UNIT 10

Adventure
ascent
challenge
equipment
expedition
guide
peak
quest
similarities
thrill

Other Nouns
brochure
career
enthusiasm
fee
funding
relief
strength
sympathy
temperature

Verbs
to fail
to give up
to involve
to provide

Adjectives
explicit
implicit

Adverbs
barely
extremely
no longer

UNIT 11

Nouns
authenticity
candidate
clue
formal
level
role model
variation
variety
wrist

Verbs
to acknowledge
to cut (someone) off
to defend
to knock
to make up (one's) mind
to put aside
to put away
to put in time
to put (someone) down
to put (someone) on
to put (something) over on (someone)
to put up (something)
to put up with (someone or something)
to hold (one's) peace
to make a point
to vote

Adjectives
non-standard
peculiar
tight

Adverb
likely

UNIT 12

Nouns
athlete
dismay
facilities
glory
honor
immortality
legend
obstacles
safety
series
site
status
symbol

Verbs
to aim
to drown
to manage to
to promote
to reflect

Adjectives
adequate
forbidden

Adverb
precisely

Expressions
hang in there
in deep water
never mind
on the ball
to pass the ball
pros and cons
swimming in (money)
your serve

VOCABULARY

Arabic numbers indicate units in In Charge 1. GS *indicates "Getting Started."*

to abandon 4
abrupt 8
absence 4
accurate 1
to acknowledge 11
to adapt 3
additional 7
adequate 12
to aim 12
allergic 6
ambiguous 4
anecdote 1
to appeal 7
appropriate 4
arbitrarily 8
archipelago 9
ascent 10
assertion 8
assessment 8
astringent 6
athlete 12
atmosphere 7
attitude 3
authenticity 11
autobiography 2
available 2

background
  (economic) 2
ban 5
bang 5
bar graph 1
barely 10
bay 9
behavior 1
bent over 6
to be somebody 2
bias 9
biography 2
birdbrain 1
black sheep 1
bookworm 1
brevity 4
brochure 10
burned 6

canal 9
candidate 11
canyon 9
capable 1
career 10

cartographer 9
casualty 5
category 4
catnap 1
challenge 10
channel 9
to clear up 6
cliff 9
clue 11
clumsy 8
coast 9
to coin 7
complicated 8
to concede 9
concerns GS
cons, and pros 12
consecutive 7
consensus 8
controversial 3
to convey 6
to correlate 1
corruption 3
costly 5
costumes 7
to cover 2
to cover up 6
credibility 2
critic 3
crocodile tears 1
to cut (someone)
  off 11

to dare 3
data 2
debate 7
to defend 11
definitive 3
delta 9
densely 9
to deny 4
to derive 3
descendant 5
destiny 7
to dig in 6
director 3
disadvantage 4
disco 7
dismay 12
display 5
dissent 7
distinctive 9

dog-tired 1
to drop out 2
to drown 12

to eat up 2
eccentric 2
edibles 6
to endanger 1
to endure 2
enthusiasm 10
equipment 10
essential 7
euphemism 7
to evolve 7
to exaggerate 9
to exert 2
expedition 10
explicit 10
explosive 5
extensive 3
extremely 10
extrovert 8

face mask 6
facilities 12
factors 6
to fail 10
failure 2
to feature 9
fee 10
festival 3
firecracker 5
firework 5
firm 4
fishy 1
to flunk 2
to focus 4
forbidden 12
formal 11
frenzy 7
funding 10
fuss 4

to gain GS
to generalize 8
geographer 9
to get (one's) way
  2
to get over 8
gist 5
to give up 10

glory 12
goose bumps 1
to go over 4
gospel 7
to grasp 1
guide 10

hang in there 12
harbor 9
headline 5
heavy metal 7
to hold (one's)
  peace 11
honor 12
humiliating 8
hypothesis 1

image 7
immortality 12
impact 3
implicit 10
to incorporate 3
in deep water 12
indelible 7
inference 5
insight 4
instruction 4
intent 1
to interact 4
to interpret 3
interpretation GS
introvert 8
to involve 10
ironic 3
isolated 5

to justify 5

to keep in 4
to keep track of 8
to keep up 4
to knock 11

to label 8
laboratory 1
leavetaking 4
legend 12
lethal 5
level 11
lighting 7
likely 11

literal 4
lobster 6
to look down on 8
lucrative 7

to make a point 11
to make up (one's)
  mind 11
to manage to 12
mapmaker 9
masterpiece 3
melancholy 7
melon 6
merit 8
to mimic 1
minority 3
misleading 9
to motivate 6

neutral 3
never mind 12
no longer 10
non-standard 11
novelist 3
nutrition 6

objective 2
obstacles 12
occasion 4
odd 5
oily 6
old-fashioned 5
on the ball 12
optimist GS
origin 5
oven 6

parrot 1
passion GS
to pass the ball 12
pattern 2
peak 10
peculiar 11
peninsula 9
to perceive 1
pessimist GS
pessimistic 3
plentiful 6
polite 6
populated 9
portion 2

VOCABULARY   **151**

potluck dinner 6
poverty 2
precisely 12
predictable 8
prejudice 2
to process 1
producer 3
prominent 9
promising 7
to promote 12
pros and cons 12
to provide 10
psychologist 8
to put aside 11
to put away 11
to put in time 11
to put (someone)
    down 11
to put (someone)
    on 11
to put (something)
    over on
    (someone) 11
to put up
    (something) 11
to put up with
    (someone or
    something) 8
pyrotechnician 5

quest 10
questionnaire 4

rap 7
rat-race 1
realist 8
to reassure 8
rebellion 3
to recycle 5
to reflect 12
reflection 7
refreshing 6
reggae 7
to reject 4
to relate 5
relief 10
reluctant 4
remarkable 5
renowned 5
repose 5
research 2
to restrict 5
to reveal 9
reward 1
risky 5
road hog 1
roasted 6
role model 11
to run into 8

safety 12
scholarship 2
screenwriter 3
scriptwriter 3
scrumptious 6
seafood 6
secret GS
sentimental 8
series 12
serve, your 12
shoreline 9
shrimp 6
signal 1
similarities 10
site 12
to sketch 9
to skip 7
soul GS
specific GS
to speculate 6
to spoil 6
sponsor 3
statistics 9
status 12
to stay away from
    8
to stick to 4
to stimulate 3
strength 10

subject (of a
    biography) 2
subjective 1
subsequent 8
suburbs 4
to suffer 2
superior 6
swamp 9
swimming in
    (money) 12
symbol 12
sympathy 10

taste 7
temperature 10
tender 2
tentative 4
to think over 8
thrill 10
thriller 3
to throw (one's
    self) into 2
tight 11
tips GS
tolerance 3
tone 4
tough 2
tradition 5
tragic 7

to transform 5
true grit 2
to tune in 4
turkey 6
to turn (become)
    5
type (kind) 8

undesirable 6
unflattering 3
unique 3
unpredictable 5

valley 9
variation 11
varied 5
variety 11
to visualize 9
to vote 11

to warm 6
well-adjusted 8
whale 1
wild-goose chase
    1
wrist 11

yogurt 6
your serve 12

zone 9

INDEX

Arabic numbers indicate units in In Charge 1. GS *indicates "Getting Started."*

From ''This Bird Has a Way with Words'' by Douglas Starr, *National Wildlife* 26, February-March 1988. Reprinted by permission of National Wildlife. 5-6; From ''Idioglossia'' by J.N., THE PEOPLE'S ALMANAC™ #2 by David Wallechinsky and Irving Wallace. Copyright © 1978 by David Wallechinsky and Irving Wallace. Reprinted by permission. 10 (listening transcript); From ''Comedy Under Control'' by Dan Goodgame, with Cosby, TIME, September 28, 1987. Copyright © 1987 Time Warner Inc. Reprinted by permission. 16; Carol Burnett, ONE MORE TIME. New York: Random House, Inc., 1986. 24; ''Diego Rivera: I Paint What I See'' from The 26th Chicago International Film Festival Catalogue, 1990. Reprinted by permission of The 26th Chicago International Film Festival. 36; From ''Fast-Leaver or Dawdler?'' by Caryl S. Avery, SELF, March 1985. 40-41; From ''A bang-up job'' by William Ecenbarger, *Chicago Tribune,* July 3, 1991. Copyright © 1991, Chicago Tribune Company, all rights reserved, used with permission. 52-53; From THE PEOPLE'S ALMANAC™ by David Wallechinsky and Irving Wallace. Copyright © 1975 by David Wallechinsky and Irving Wallace. All Rights Reserved. Reprinted by permission. 72; From ''Personality's Part and Parcel'' by Paul Chance, PSYCHOLOGY TODAY, Vol. 22, No. 4, April 1988. Copyright © 1988 by PSYCHOLOGY TODAY. Reprinted by permission of PSYCHOLOGY TODAY Magazine. (Sussex Publishers, Inc.) 88-89; Place Maps by Cheryl Simon, PSYCHOLOGY TODAY, November 1987. Copyright © 1987 by PSYCHOLOGY TODAY. Reprinted by permission of PSYCHOLOGY TODAY Magazine. (Sussex Publishers, Inc.) 100-101; Text only, abridged, from IDITAROD: The Last Great Race On Earth brochure. Reprinted by permission of the Iditarod Trail Committee, Inc. 120-121; ''The Pocketbook Game'' from LIKE ONE OF THE FAMILY by Alice Childress. Copyright © 1956. Renewed 1984 by Alice Childress. Used by permission of Flora Roberts, Inc. 124-125; From ''45 Years in Culture and Creative Writing'' by Gwendolyn Brooks, EBONY, November 1990. Reprinted by permission of Gwendolyn Brooks. 132-133; ''I Walked Off Eight-And-A-Half Pounds'' by Holly Reich, NEW WOMAN, May 1990. 145.

Photography

Unless otherwise acknowledged, all photographs are the property of ScottForesman. Page abbreviations are as follows (T) top, (B) bottom, (L) left, (R) right, (C) center. Alan Oddie/Photo Edit 1; Michael Goldman/Sisyphus 5 and 6; Alan and Sandy Carey, Bozeman, MT, Lawrence Manning/H. Armstrong Roberts, H. Armstrong Roberts, Amthor/Zefa/H. Armstrong Roberts 7T to B; Frink/Waterhouse/H. Armstrong Roberts, E.R. Degginger/H. Armstrong Roberts, P. Burd/H. Armstrong Roberts 9LC to R; John D. Cunningham/Visuals Unlimited 10T; San Diego Historical Society, Union/Tribune Collection 10B; Scott Shulman/Shooting Star, AP/Wide World Photos, Stephen Harvey/Shooting Star, Donald Dietz/Sony Classical 15TR; The White House Historical Association 15CL; S.S./Shooting Star 16; AP/Wide World Photos, AP/Wide World Photos, Shooting Star, Lee Salem/Shooting Star, Photofest, Eddie Sanderson/Shooting Star 22TR; Robert Frerck/Odyssey 22BR; Kobal Collection/Superstock 24T; Courtesy Will Rogers Memorial 25BL and R; Photofest 27LC; AP/Wide World Photos 27BL; AP/Wide World Photos, AP/Wide World Photos, Photofest 28CL to R; William Claxton/Kobal Collection/Superstock 29TR; Photofest 29LC; Kobal Collection/Superstock 30; Photofest 31; Photofest 34; AP/Wide World Photos 35; San Francisco Examiner 36; John Forasté/Brown University 48; Shostal/Superstock, AP/Wide World Photos 51TC and R; Kevin Horan 52T; AP/Wide World Photos 52B; Courtesy Zambelli Internationale 53; Courtesy AFCO Industries 58; D. Logan/H. Armstrong Roberts, Camerique/H. Armstrong Roberts 63BC and R; David O. Houston/Bruce Coleman, Inc., New York, H. Armstrong Roberts 64RC and B; Photography by Milt and Joan Mann, Cameramann International 65TC; H. Armstrong Roberts 70; Camerique/H. Armstrong Roberts 75C; Elliot Landy/Magnum Photos 75B; Shooting Star 76RC and B; Shooting Star, Bill Levy/Janice Joplin 77RC and B; AP/Wide World Photos, Dagmar/Shooting Star 78CL and R; King/Gamma Liaison 80; Yoram Kahana/Shooting Star 82; AP/Wide World Photos, AP/Wide World Photos, Frank Driggs Collection 84TR to C; Giraudon/Art Resource 92; Carl Roessler/FPG International 105; Warren Morgan/H. Armstrong Roberts 111; AP/Wide World Photos, AP/Wide World Photos 112; AP/Wide World Photos 118; Camerique/H. Armstrong Roberts 122; AP/Wide World Photos 132; UPI/Bettman 136; AP/Wide World Photos, AP/Wide World Photos, 137; AP/Wide World Photos 138; Danny Feld/Shooting Star 139; Michael Neveus/H. Armstrong Roberts 145.

Illustrations

Rob Porazinski 2; George Ulrich 3; Rob Porazinski 4; Eldon Doty 8; Benton Mahan 11; George Ulrich 12; Benton Mahan 14; Randy Verougstraete 18; Eldon Doty 23; Rob Porazinski 27; Rob Porazinski 28; Rob Porazinski 30; Stephanie O'Shaughnessy 32; Randy Verougstraete 37T, Rob Porazinski 37B; George Ulrich 39; Richard Erickson 40; Richard Erickson 41; Benton Mahan 42; Randy Verougstraete 44; George Ulrich 45; George Ulrich 46; Stephanie O'Shaughnessy 47; Randy Verougstraete 49; Randy Verougstraete 55; George Ulrich 59; Benton Mahan 60; George Ulrich 61; Eldon Doty 62; Benton Mahan 63; Eldon Doty 65; Randy Verougstraete 66; Eldon Doty 67; Eldon Doty 68; George Ulrich 71; Stephanie O'Shaughnessy 72; Benton Mahan 73; George Ulrich 74; Eldon Doty 75; Stephanie O'Shaughnessy 87; Eldon Doty 88; Eldon Doty 90; George Ulrich 91; Eldon Doty 93; George Ulrich 95; Benton Mahan 97; George Ulrich 100; George Ulrich 107; Eldon Doty 108; Turner Fair III 109; Eldon Doty 115; George Ulrich 117; George Ulrich 119; Eldon Doty 121; George Ulrich 124; George Ulrich 126; Eldon Doty 127; Stephanie O'Shaughnessy 129; George Ulrich 130; Benton Mahan 135.